NEVER GIVE UP

Overcome Life's Challenges and Achieve Success

NILESH SATHE

Popular Prakashan

www.popularprakashan.com

Published by
Harsha Bhatkal for
POPULAR PRAKASHAN PVT. LTD.
301, Mahalaxmi Chambers
22, Bhulabhai Desai Road
Mumbai - 400 026

First Published 2021

(4532)
ISBN: 978-81-950882-4-9

Cover design and layout: Anjali Sawant

PRINTED IN INDIA
by Saurabh Printers (P) Ltd.
Plot No. 67 A-68, Ecotech, Ext. I
Kasna, Greater Noida-201306 (U.P)

Dedicated to

My mother who shaped my personality and built my character
and
My wife who always stood beside me in difficult times

Contents

Foreword – S B Mathur, Former Chairman, LIC of India vii

Preface ix

I. My Childhood: A Combination of Struggle and Values 1

II. College Days and My Banking Experience 19

III. Initial Grooming in LIC 33

IV. Nagpur – Pune – Solapur 47

V. Aamar Shonar Kolkata 61

VI. Mumbai – My Love 71

VII. Duty First 105

VIII. Five Golden Years in 'Antariksha' 117

IX. Delhi: Dreadful Days 135

X. Learning Curve – LIC Mutual Fund and My Fight with Cancer 161

About the Author 181

Contents

About the Author

Foreword

I am a firm believer in the fact that the life story of all men and women provides the greatest level of thrill, excitement and mystery surpassing all drama exhibited on celluloid or OTT in today's crazy world. If you persuade a person to tell his or her life story with full sincerity, the story that emerges will be greater than what any entertainment medium dishes out to us day in and day out.

The author, in his book *Never Give Up*, proves the above point beyond any doubt. I started browsing through the book hoping that I would skip some parts and get a general idea of the contents to be able to write a foreword. However, once I opened the book and started reading, I was completely mesmerized and read each page with my antennas wide open. The narrative comes straight from the heart, without any colouring, something not very common in the era of social media where truth and falsehood blend without any sense of guilt. I am sure everyone who reads this book will be spellbound with the flow of events so beautifully describing every facet of the authors' personality, his fears, anxiety, struggle, and his desire to face these with determination and a proactive and positive mindset.

The journey in the corporate world, rising to top leadership position, the efforts, personal trauma and the challenges the author faced are described in simple but very impactful words. The description of his fight with cancer is explicit and the experience will be a source of strength to all those who are unfortunate victims of this dreadful disease.

Never Give Up is a must-read not only for those who want to make a success in the corporate world as also for those who are afflicted with major diseases and become recluse out of despondency. My friend and former colleague Mr Nilesh Sathe has done society a great service by penning his experiences in this book. I wish him all the success.

– S B Mathur
Former Chairman
LIC of India

Preface

Why did I write an autobiography? I am not a luminary like a politician or a sportsperson or an artist known to millions of people. I am a common man with an uncommon 'Never Say Die' attitude. Like most other people, I had struggled and worked hard all my life dealing with difficulties and obstacles, as best as I could. Like most people, my life was also full of worries, anxieties and problems which I tried to get over with a positive frame of mind.

It is said, 'When the going gets tough, the tough get going' and it happened in my life as well. I had to face the agony of my father's death when I was just four, had my primary education in villages which had no electricity. My mother had to undergo a cancer surgery in the year of my matriculation. As if this was not enough, while facing challenges in office, I too suffered from cancer and had to undergo three surgeries in three years...

It was an 'enjoyable' though challenging journey of my life, which I thought of sharing with the readers. Initially I worked in a bank for over five years. This was followed by a job in Life Insurance Corporation of India (LIC) for three decades, reaching the top position of Executive Director, then as Director and CEO of LIC Nomura Mutual Fund Asset Management Company (AMC) for three years and lastly as an Insurance Regulator for four years. It gave me a 360 degree view of the Financial Sector. I worked with dedication and devotion. I always tried to find easier ways of doing things. Fast decision making and tactfully solving problems were my forte.

My character was built by my mother who was a school teacher while my wife stood beside me like a rock in all my challenging situations in life and especially during my fight with cancer. I owe them a lot.

It's an honest account of my life story. At some places, names have been changed to protect privacy but the events are factual.

I am thankful to Harsha Bhatkal and his team at Popular Prakashan, Mumbai for releasing the book in record time. I thank Dr Preeti Shirodkar, Mumbai for helping me edit the manuscript.

The book will help the readers to boldly face challenges in life and develop a 'Never Give Up' attitude.

– Nilesh Sathe

I

My Childhood: A Combination of Struggle and Values

I was born in Nagpur in 1957. I have no memory of the first five years of my life. My knowledge of that period of my life is based on what I have heard from my mother or from my sister, who was elder to me by a year and a half. My mother was a housewife and my father was an architect with the Town Planning Department of the Government of Maharashtra. Unfortunately, I can't recall any memories of my father since I was barely four years old when he passed away.

In 1958-59, my father was transferred from Nagpur to Mumbai (formerly Bombay), where we lived in the Government colony, Bandra. Before moving to Mumbai, he had constructed a small five room house in Shankar Nagar, Nagpur. My mother, a matriculate before marriage, but always eager to study further, completed her graduation in 1959. During that time, my father was selected by the Government to go to London for a year to study low-cost housing and then he had to move to London a year thereafter. He was permitted to move there along with his family. My mother, who was an arts graduate by then, thought of completing a secondary teachers' course which would enable her to join any school as a secondary school teacher. Since she was already running a private nursery for kids in Bandra and had a liking for children's education, she decided to join a Montessori course too. She thought she might get a job at a Montessori when we move to London. Since doing these courses from Nagpur was easy, it was essential for her to move to Nagpur along with my sister and myself for a year.

My mother was progressing well in her studies at the Sevasadan Institute, Nagpur. Around this time, my father, who was in Mumbai, thought of getting a health check-up at JJ Hospital since he was to leave for London soon. During the check-up, he was diagnosed with kidney stones. The doctor advised him to get a surgery done to remove the stones.

We came down to Mumbai for his surgery at JJ Hospital on 14 October 1961. Unfortunately, the surgery was unsuccessful and he breathed his last on the operation table itself. He was just thirty-two years old. Needless to say, his passing was a great shock to our family.

After my father's death, we could have continued living in the Government quarters in Bandra but my mother was not keen to take up the benefit of Government service on compassionate grounds. The thought of staying alone in Mumbai, with two small children of ages six and four, was daunting. She decided to move back to Nagpur and complete the two courses she was pursuing. Soon thereafter, we moved to Nagpur permanently. In due course my mother appeared for the secondary teachers' course and the Montessori exams and topped in both the exams.

During that time, she accidently came across an article on Taratai Modak, a revolutionary educationist and a social worker who had started Vikaswadi, an institute for the development of *adivasis* (tribals) in Kosbad, Thane district. Taratai had started a Teachers' Diploma Course for tribal girls in Vikaswadi but the college was facing acute shortage of teachers. The article on Taratai made a deep impact on my mother and she instantly wrote to Taratai about her desire to join as a teacher in the institute. Soon she received a reply inviting her to join the academic session starting in June 1962. We then shifted to Kosbad Hill.

There was no electricity in Kosbad and this was something new for us. Taratai had sent across two lanterns and a glass kerosene lamp for the time being. My mother lit the lamps and by doing so, she illuminated our house and our lives forever. I started my schooling in Class I. The school was in the adjoining building. I used to leave for school only after hearing the school bell.

Every evening there would be a prayer meeting where most of the students, teachers and office staff would assemble. Usually Taratai would speak a few words after the prayer. Sometimes she would assign a topic to the students for them to speak on the next day. This was to encourage the students to speak in front of an audience, overcome stage fear and develop oratory skills. One evening she announced that the following day, five students either from Class I or Class II will speak on 'My pet animal'. I volunteered. I prepared my speech on a parrot and spoke on the subject the next day on stage without any fear. My speech was excellent as compared to my other friends but when the result was announced, my name wasn't mentioned. I was shocked and very unhappy.

My mother was also present when I spoke on the subject. After reaching home I asked her, "Why did I not get the prize although I spoke better than the others?" She said, "Taratai liked your speech. I was standing next to her. She wanted to give you the prize. I objected because, Nilesh you should know that parrot is a bird while the subject was, 'My pet animal'."

I learnt the first lesson of my life — understand the given subject well and don't stand in front of an audience without being fully prepared. This lesson I follow to this day. I never speak extempore.

My school teacher Mr Patil was greatly pleased with my studies. I scored well in the mid-year examination. He was so happy that he met my mother and expressed his desire to tutor me for Class II along with my Class I studies. This would help me to go to Class III the next year, skipping Class II; I would get a 'double promotion'. Under his guidance and intense tutoring, I appeared for my Class

I and Class II exams and in the next academic year I was promoted to Class III directly.

Taratai and her friend Anutai Wagh, who later headed Vikaswadi, used to play rummy every Sunday after lunch for an hour or two. One day Taratai asked my mother to send me to her house after lunch. My mother knew that they used to play cards after lunch and was reluctant to send me there as playing cards in those days was a social taboo. She could not decline Taratai's request but with a lot of reluctance she allowed me to go. When they were playing cards, Taratai would give me some easy mathematical problems to solve. She would also make me count the points of the loser and keep an account of the score. At the end of the game I would total up and announce the winner of that day by the number of points scored. I also used to check the sequence of the cards. It was great fun. In the process, my interest and liking for the mathematics deepened.

Sometime during those days, I developed a pain in my right ear and whenever my mother cleaned my ear with a cotton bud, pus would ooze out. We visited Dr Joshi at Dahanu who asked me to eat a raw egg daily as he thought that it might be due to weakness. He also asked me to come thrice a week to take an injection, which may have been an antibiotic or steroid, I am not sure. There was no physician in Kosbad who could administer an injection. Obviously, it was necessary for me to visit him at Dahanu thrice a week. After a couple of visits, my mother started sending me alone. The bus which used to come from Kosbad would reach Dahanu and after 20 minutes or so, would return to Kosbad again. I would get off at Dahanu, rush to Dr Joshi who would quickly give me the injection, offer me a candy and then I would run immediately to catch the returning bus. I never missed the bus. In spite of continuous treatment for almost six months, there was no sign of improvement and the infection in my right ear did not clear out. Finally, after my examinations were over, I was brought to Mumbai, I had a tonsillectomy which cured the infection.

My mother always kept us engaged in either studies or household chores. She would make us wipe the glass lanterns shade with ash. We learnt the skill of handling glass with care and this also helped us improve our motor skills. We always had an early dinner post which my mother, in the light of lanterns, would study till late hours. She did her MA in Marathi and Sanskrit during our two years' stay in Kosbad.

Soon we had to leave Kosbad for Vangaon which was about twenty kilometres from Kosbad. At Vangaon, a school started by one Mr Kelkar had no teacher to teach mathematics to Class XI students. It was also going to be the first batch of students to pass out from the school. He requested Taratai to send a suitable teacher for this purpose. Taratai found my mother to be the most suitable teacher for this job. Though my mother had studied mathematics only up to her matriculation (HSC) which in those days was eleven years of schooling, she was good at it. Taratai put forth this suggestion to my mother. My mother accepted it as a challenge and we left for Vangaon for the next academic session starting in June 1964 when I was in Class IV and my elder sister (Tai) was in Class V.

In Vangaon, we rented a modest two-room accommodation in a *chawl*. My maternal grandmother who lived in Amravati was diagnosed with cancer and around September, we got a telegram from her urging us to visit Amravati. We soon reached Amravati where my grandmother was counting her last days. She was actually waiting to meet my mother and within a few days, she passed away. My mother, in the meanwhile, had come across an advertisement for a vacancy of a Family Welfare Officer in Amravati. She applied for it and was selected. We decided to shift to Amravati from the next academic session. My maternal grandmother (Gore by surname) owned some twenty acres of land at Shirajgaon (Band), which was about twenty kilometres from Amravati. My mother's brother, Purushottam alias Baban Gore was in the army. He was a commissioned officer by then. Her younger brother Bandu, was fourteen years old. The agricultural land was given for tilling to someone who used to cultivate *jowar* (sorghum) and hand over half of the proceeds to my grandmother. After the death of my grandmother, my mother was the sole responsible person to look after the agricultural land. Had she continued in Vangaon which was over eight hundred kilometres away, it would have been impossible to look after the agricultural land. Moreover, since she was born and brought up in Amaravati, she must have had a natural inclination to be suitably engaged at Amravati.

Whatever may be the reason, we definitely benefited from the change in the form of having electric lights once again. We rented a two-room house on Badnera Road and the house had electricity. We were very excited that we no longer had to study in the light of a lantern. But my mother said, "Now since electricity is here, you should study harder and secure more marks in school. You will find many good students in your class here. They should never have the impression that since you studied in a village, you cannot compete with them." I was admitted to Class V at Samarth Vidyalaya, Amravati.

My mother had a desire to become a school teacher for which the qualification of B.Ed. (Bachelor of Education) was a must. She took up a job as Family Welfare Officer for a year and saved up enough money to fulfil her desire and joined Shivaji College in Amravati for the B.Ed. course the following year. She passed the exam in first division ranking second in the order of merit.

There was a very renowned school in Nagpur called Hadas High School. The principal of the school Mr P R Joshi was always in search of good teachers. When he came to know that my mother had the requisite qualification to become a secondary school teacher, he offered her the position of a teacher in the school. I also had a special sentiment attached to the school since the architecture of the school was designed by my father and my paternal grandfather had supervised the construction of the building free of cost while we were staying in Nagpur before 1960. Moreover, we had our own house in Nagpur. We therefore decided to shift to Nagpur and in the academic year of 1967-68, I was admitted to Class VII and Tai to Class VIII at Hadas High School where Aai joined as a secondary school teacher. The unique feature about the plan for the school designed by my father Late Bhaskar Vishnu Sathe was that it was well ventilated and allowed a lot of light into the classrooms as it was F-shaped and had a swimming tank. It was probably the only school then, at least in Maharashtra, to have one for the students to learn swimming. I used to take pride in showing to my friends my father's and grandfather's names displayed at the entrance of the school.

There used to be a common exam all over Maharashtra for students studying in Class VII for a high school entrance scholarship. Many students from our class appeared for the exam and sixteen of them got a scholarship of ₹20 per month. I was one of them. When my school fee was ₹8 for the whole year, a scholarship of ₹20 per month was quite a substantial amount.

I started taking part in co-curricular activities and joined *kho-kho* team. I joined a classical music class nearby and studied up to *Madhyama* level. I had a melodious voice. I was selected in our school music team for group songs and we got an opportunity to sing songs in a radio program for children called *Bal-Vihar*. I used to take part in children's dramas played in *Bal-Vihar*. I passed the audition test and started getting contracts from All India Radio (AIR) for participating in radio dramas. I became a radio artist and was in such good demand that there was no month when my name was not heard on AIR either as a participant in a song or as an artist in a play.

My mother, being a school teacher, was very particular that we learnt the right morals and virtues in life. From our early age she tried to imbibe these qualities in us. I took part in sports and co-curricular activities like singing, acting during my school days. I was however never in the top ten in academics although I never missed the first division. She always used to tell me, "In *Kho-Kho*, when you know that you are out, you should own up and leave the playing field. Avoid the temptation of doing wrong."

Character building mostly happens during the formative years and adolescence and it takes many years to build character. It happens brick by brick. One incident during my school days helped me build one brick of my character. I was in Class VIII A while my mother was the English teacher for Class VIII C. Mid-year exams were over and she brought four to five bundles of answer papers for evaluation. Placing them on the table, she had gone to the vegetable market. Out of curiosity, I tried to find which class and section's papers she had brought for evaluation and to my surprise, I found that my section's English papers had come to her for evaluation. I was curious to know the marks I had scored. I untied the bundle. My roll number was 38. I kept on turning the answer papers and found that the paper of roll number 38 was missing. I got disheartened and tied the string (*sutali*) exactly the way it was tied before and placed the bundle back on the table.

After some time, my mother came home, we had dinner and it was time for her to start evaluating the papers. I was studying in the adjacent room. She called me and asked, "Nilesh, did you unbundle the papers of your class?" I honestly replied, "Yes, but how did you come to know about it? I had retied *sutali* exactly the same way it was tied before." She said, "I happen to know child psychology. Once you know that your section's papers have come to me for evaluation, you may be tempted to correct a few mistakes in the paper which you might have made at the time of examination. I have, hence, already checked your paper in the school itself and have kept it in my school locker." I said, "I didn't want to make any corrections but was curious to know the marks I scored. Please tell me my marks."

She said, "I won't tell you that. You will know them when the other forty-nine students of your class know their marks. Never get tempted to do the wrong things in life. Honesty is the best virtue. The mind is weak. You need to practice how to keep it under control."

Such incidents have had an ever-lasting impression on me. She kept a close watch on our activities, our friends and our language. Tai passed her SSC (Secondary School Certificate) in 1970 in first division and joined G S College of Commerce and Economics for pre-university.

During Ganesh festival every year, Mr Madhukar Dantale, an officer at State Bank and a resident of our colony, used to write and direct a one act play for children. I participated and it was great fun to practice the play at his home in Shankar Nagar. My interest in dramas was at its peak when I was in the Class X. That year, the college students from our locality, Shankar Nagar, decided to stage a three-act play, a farcical one named *'Kaka Kishacha'* (Kisha's uncle) written by Shyam Phadke, a noted Marathi farcical drama writer. I used to watch the practice, although I had no role in the drama. The drama was to be staged on a Friday, during the ten days' Ganesh festival on the grounds of the Municipal School where a stage was erected. Our school began at 7:00 am every Saturday and at 10:30 am on weekdays. My mother used to wake up at 5:00 am on Saturday. Since the play was scheduled for Friday evening, she asked my sister and me to return home by midnight. When the second act was over, it suddenly started raining and the third act started only at 11:50 pm. I knew that it would take another thirty minutes for the drama to be over but was reluctant to go home without watching the climax of the play. My sister, however, left for home after the second act.

As soon as the drama was over, I quickly ran to our house and it took me hardly five to seven minutes to reach home. We lived in three rooms of our house while the remaining two rooms were let out to tenants. My grandfather and I slept in the front room, my mother (*Aai*) and my sister (*Tai*) slept in the back room. Behind that room was the kitchen. I called my grandfather in a soft voice and requested him to open the door to which he replied, "Ask your mother." I realised that the situation was bad. I went near the window of the room where my mother was sleeping and said, "Aai I have reached. Please open the door. I know that I am late but I will not do so again."

She asked me, "At what time were you supposed to be home?"

"At 12 midnight."

"What is the time now?"

"Maybe 12:30 half past midnight."

"Now stay in the courtyard. I will open the door only at 5:00 am when I wake up."

I kept on requesting her but she stood firm. After a while, my grandfather said to my mother, "Prabha, you may punish him but open the door and let Nilesh in." She asked me, "What punishment do you want?"

"Whatever you decide, but open the door now."

She got up, went to the kitchen and brought something. She asked me to put my left hand in through the window bars. I thought that she would hit me on my palm with a ruler or *belan* but she scalded my hand with a cindered *agarbatti* (incense stick). I pulled my hand back in agony. I heard her saying, "The door is open. Come inside and apply some oil on your hand. You will always remember the importance of being on time. You have no reason to keep others waiting for you."

Truthfulness and punctuality became my habit. I don't remember being late either to office or to any meetings.

The next academic year was very important for me. I had to appear for matriculation. It was our first batch of HSC (matriculation after eleven years of schooling). Till then our school had SSC only (ten years of schooling). The syllabus for Class XI was really tough. Physics, Chemistry and Maths were very difficult subjects. Even the teachers spoke about it. We got scared. The teachers had no experience of teaching the Class XI. Maths was my pet subject hence I was sure to understand it based on the clarifications in the book. I could somehow manage with Chemistry but in the first terminal exam when I scored just above the passing marks in Physics, I could foresee my future. I got worried. I decided to be on a lookout for Physics tuition. Personal tuitions were very costly. I did not want to put more financial burden on my mother who was finding it difficult to make ends meet, being the sole earning member of our family. Aai always used to say, "Think before you spend. Buy only if it is necessary." They were the words of a person who was neither poor nor a miser but not extravagant either.

I remembered Jayant Tutorial Classes (JTC) run by Professor Dattaji Didolkar. The classes were for Physics, Chemistry and Maths for college students from pre-university (which was the equivalent of Class XI in school) to B.Sc. Dattaji was director of JTC and he was famous in Nagpur as someone who devoted his life to RSS as a *Pracharak* in Tamil Nadu for many years. Before becoming a *Pracharak*, he was a gold medalist in M.Sc. (Physics). By the time I thought of joining JTC for Physics even my mid-year exam was over and I had marginally improved my performance in Physics but not to my satisfaction. I was worried. Hardly four months were left for the final exam. I discussed my fears with my mother who agreed to my proposal of enrolling at JTC for Physics. Almost half the academic session of JTC was over. I wanted to join classes of Physics only. But when I met the clerk at JTC, he told me that I would be required to pay full fees for all the three subjects because subject wise admissions were not given.

I informed my mother about this rule, she asked me to meet Mr Didolkar, the Director. I was going to JTC every day to meet Dattaji but I was unable to meet him as he was always surrounded by students. Finally, the third time I returned without meeting him, my mother advised me to write an application mentioning my difficulty and leave it on his table before he came to JTC. Accordingly, I wrote an application requesting him to allow me admission only for one subject, Physics, and also that the fees be charged for one subject only.

That day when I went to JTC, Dattaji had come a bit early and was sitting in the office. He called me and said, "I have noticed you for the last two three days. What do you want?"

I gave him my application. He glared at me and asked, "What does your father do?" I said, "He was an architect and died when I was four."

"What does your mother do?"

"She is a teacher in Hadas High School."

He further asked me my score in PCM subjects in mid-year exams. He also asked me about my marks in Class X, the reason behind joining classes so late and whether I knew that the syllabus of pre-science was slightly different from that of Class XI etc. On hearing me, he wrote a remark on my application. "Admitted only for Physics. Take fees only for one subject at half rate." He asked me to give that note to the clerk and asked me to go to class, as he was going to take Physics class in a few minutes. I told him that I had not brought any cash for payment of fees nor did I have a notebook. He said, "Don't worry. Ask for a few pages form any student. Go fast. I am coming."

I was extremely delighted that Dattaji had allowed me to join class at half fee for only one subject.

I went to the classroom on the first floor. All the students sitting there were college students wearing full trousers. As I entered, they saw me wearing half pants, they started shouting, "This class is not for school goers." I wanted to occupy a seat at the back bench. But a student noticing my short stature offered me his seat in the first row and he moved to the last bench. The student sitting next to me gave me two papers from his exercise book to take down notes. Nobody teased me or jeered at me thereafter and I felt at home rather than feeling lonely.

Dattaji was a great teacher. Very soon I developed an interest in Physics and became confident of scoring good marks in Physics in HSC. After two months or so, the prelim exams were over and I scored good marks in all the subjects including Physics.

The board exams were to be held after two months and I was gaining momentum in my studies.

We occasionally used to watch movies in those days. Generally, after the final examination my mother used to allow us to go for a movie. In 1971-72, a new cinema hall named Saroj Talkies (now Sudama) was built and the first movie released there was Anand. Yes, it was the same Anand in which Rajesh Khanna died of cancer and Amitabh Bachchan who acted as Dr Bhaskar Banerjee, helplessly watched his death. The new talkies was very close to our house and both the talkies and the movie were being highly appreciated, as such one evening, Aai and Tai decided to go for the evening show. I did not join them as I had to study for my upcoming HSC exam. On coming back Tai narrated the story to me in brief and I decided to watch it after the exam.

The very next day after watching the film, Aai noticed a tumour in her left breast. A biopsy was done which showed that it was malignant. We decided to shift her to Mumbai and get her operated at Tata Memorial Cancer Hospital (TMCH). It was decided that initially she would stay at Colony Nursing Home Matunga owned by Dr Ajit Phadke who was related to us.

Since our exam was approaching fast, Aai advised us to carry all the necessary books for study. We reached Colony Nursing Home. A separate room was kept for Aai. I along with Tai stayed at Dr Ajit Phadke's residence which was in the adjacent building.

The entire first floor belonged to Ajit Kaka. It had seven to eight rooms, a huge dining table where at least ten to twelve persons could sit. There were two cooks and a servant. They were like family members. Two weeks passed but still there were no signs of getting an appointment at TMCH. Dr Prafulla Desai, a surgeon in TMCH was a friend of Ajit Kaka. He was trying to get the date of the operation fixed quickly but was not succeeding. My exams were just a fortnight away and although I was studying, I was in two minds whether to appear for the exam or not, as I was not ready to leave Aai.

A few days later Ajit Kaka called Tai and myself to his cabin and handed over two tickets for the Dadar-Nagpur Express leaving the next day. He said, “HSC is an important exam. We are all here to take care of Prabhatai. You should go to Nagpur, appear for the exam and pass with good marks. God forbid, if something untoward happens, you will be able to get a job if you score good marks in HSC.” We touched his feet, took his blessings and came to meet Aai.

Aai knew that our tickets were booked. As she embraced us and moved her frail fingers through our hair, both of us were in tears. She said, “Don’t cry. You need to be strong when a calamity strikes. I know that you are leaving for Nagpur to appear for your exams. You are intelligent enough to pass with good marks. Be cool, be patient. Nothing will happen to me. I will come home soon after the cancer surgery. But God forbid, in case I die, Nilima you are the elder one and have a great responsibility. Don’t give up education. You may mortgage our house in Nagpur, raise some money but I want both of you to be at least graduates. And Nilima, you promise me that you won’t marry before Nilesh completes his education. I have some gold in my locker. If the same is required to be sold off, do so but if not, divide it equally. I have already got the house transferred in Nilesh’s name hence raising loan against the property won’t be difficult. I will come back fully recovered, don’t worry but one must be prepared for any contingency. Take care of each other.”

Although we could not prevent tears rolling down our cheeks, our respect for her increased many folds. There was determination in her words and no tears in her eyes. What a great and brave soul!

We reached Nagpur. Fortunately, my final practical exam for Physics and Chemistry were over before we had left for Mumbai. I had missed Dattaji’s Physics tutorials and wanted to catch up on the lost portion. I went to a friend to pick up notes. He told me that Dattaji had called me to see him in his office. I thought that he would scold me for missing the classes although he had given me a huge concession in fees. But that was not to happen. On seeing me, he left his seat, came to me, patted me on my head and said, "Your friend had told me about your Aai's illness. How is she now? When is the operation? Did you get the notes? Don't worry. You study from the notes and come personally to me if you have any difficulty. You will score first class in Physics, I am sure." His words of compassion, wisdom and solace gave me strength which was what I needed the most at that moment. As I was leaving, the office clerk called me and gave me some cash. When I asked him the reason, he said, "Dattaji has ordered a full refund of your fees." What a greatness! What a magnanimity! I was speechless. I went back to Dattaji, touched his feet and thanked him for the refund. He gave me some notes which he had not distributed in the class. He blessed me and said, "All will be well, Nilesh. Don't worry. Write your exam well."

In the meanwhile, we were informed about Aai's operation at TMCH. When we heard her voice on the phone after a long time, our joy knew no bounds. We were eager to see Aai as early as possible. Although my examination was over, there were fifteen days left for Tai's examination to be over.

As soon as Tai's examination was over, we went to Mumbai and stayed with Dr Ajit kaka. Aai was recovering well. She was advised to rest for another fifteen to twenty days. Ajit kaka had a huge collection of books and during that period we read as many books as we could. We also did some sightseeing. We visited various places of interest in Mumbai like the aquarium, *Ranicha Baug, Girgaon Chowpatty* etc. We also visited our relatives and well-wishers in Mumbai. I was now eager to return to Nagpur as my HSC result was around the corner. Finally, before leaving Mumbai, Aai had to be taken to TMCH for her check-up. Both of us accompanied her.

It was for the first time ever that I was visiting TMCH. The OPD was so crowded that there was no seating left, even for the patients. A patient was accompanied by at least three to four of his relatives. Some patients having tubes dangling from their nostrils were waiting for their turn. Patients of all ages ranged from infants to elderly. Some patients who had oral cancer had a portion of their face removed. I was really scared at the terrible sights around me. I was standing in the queue to get a file (containing the patient's history) holding a card having my mother's File Number AD 2255. Finally, my number came after an hour and the attendant asked me to give the file to the nurse who was standing outside the cabin of Dr Prafulla Desai. We moved near the cabin. The nurse asked us to wait outside the doctor's cabin for about half an hour as the doctor had still not come to the cabin.

Meanwhile, Aai's chest X-ray was done. Dr Desai came and soon thereafter, the nurse started calling out the patient's name that had come for consultation. He was so quick that each patient was coming out within five minutes. Finally, my mother's name was called. We went inside. He saw the X-ray plate and asked my mother how she was feeling. He wrote something on the file and the nurse called another patient in. It was all over in three to four minutes. When we came out, the nurse said, a few medicines were prescribed and some date in August (three months later) was given for the next check-up. She also advised us to collect our railway concession forms (cancer patients were charged one-fourth the ticket price and one attendant accompanying the patient was charged three-fourth the ticket price. This facility continues even now. Thanks to the Indian Railways). When we reached Colony Nursing Home, all of us were exhausted, physically and mentally both. In the evening when Ajit Kaka came, he saw the file and said, "Tai, you have recovered well and now you may go back to Nagpur. I will ask my Assistant to book your train tickets." We were very glad that we could return to Nagpur with our beloved mother. There was a sparkle on our faces. We had no words to thank Dr Ajit Phadke for his support.

We reached Nagpur. My HSC result was out. I had passed with sixty-eight per cent marks. I was surprised to find that the words of Dattaji had come true. I had scored exactly sixty per cent marks in Physics. I was delighted.

I had a special interest in Maths. I wanted to become a professor of mathematics. I therefore decided to take admission in the Institute of Science for Maths, Statistics and Physics in B.Sc. Part I. Getting admission there was quite easy as many of the students who scored even less marks than me had decided to join engineering college. Days were simply flying. In August 1972 Tai accompanied Aai to TMCH for a quarterly check-up. Fortunately, nothing adverse was noticed and the next appointment was in the first week of November. This time, I accompanied her. While we were in the Colony Nursing Home for a day, I came to know of the sad demise of two close relatives of Ajit Kaka who were operated for cancer a few months before Aai. One of them was a lady patient who had two school going daughters. She was operated for breast cancer two months before Aai, but it was found that the cancer was spreading and hence she was operated again but unfortunately, she died. This information left me in extreme shock. When we went to TMCH for an appointment of Dr Desai, looking at the condition of the patients, my heart sank. I thought God forbid, if something unpleasant happens to my mother and I am forced to quit my study, I would not be able to continue my studies privately since to obtain a B.Sc. degree, you need to go to college. Did I make a wrong decision in joining a B.Sc. course? I should have joined the commerce stream in which college attendance is not compulsory. I made up my mind and on returning to Nagpur informed Aai about my decision to quit B.Sc. and join B.Com. She asked me to meet Principal Tokhi of G S College of Commerce (where my Tai was studying) and take his advice since more than half of the academic session was over.

The next day I met Mr Tokhi. Tai was also with me. Looking at my HSC mark sheet, he said, "Nilesh, not many students with such high scores come here to join the B.Com. course. But now since November is coming to an end, if you take admission in B.Com. Part I, you may find it difficult to score good marks. I suggest you to take admission in pre-university commerce so that your foundation becomes strong. And once you score a first class in pre-university, there will be no looking back. I will admit you and give a full fee waiver." I was deeply grateful for his advice. In the next two to three days, I moved from the Institute of Science to join G S College of Commerce where I studied for the next four years. The college was instrumental in shaping my personality.

Lessons Learnt...

- Understand the given subject well and don't stand in front of an audience without being fully prepared.
- When you know you are wrong, own up and correct your mistake instead of hiding it. Avoid the temptation of doing wrong.
- Truthfulness and punctuality are important habits to cultivate. Honesty is the best virtue. The mind is weak. You need to practice how to keep it under control.
- Character building mostly happens during the formative years and adolescence and it takes many years to build character. It happens brick by brick. Teach your children the right morals and virtues in life.
- Always remember the importance of being on time. You have no reason to keep others waiting for you.
- Think before you spend.

II

College Days and My Banking Experience

I began attending G S College and found that the subjects in the commerce course were relatively easy and interesting. I had lost almost six months but I picked up the subjects quite fast. Tai went with Aai for the next quarterly check up in February 1973. Fortunately, nothing adverse was detected. I appeared for the pre-university exam and in due course, when the result was out, I had passed in first division with distinction in two subjects. Tokhi sir's advice proved right. My foundation in commerce became solid because I did pre-university. It gave me a lot of confidence and I was sure to pass B.Com., even privately, without going to college if something untoward happened in the future. Fortunately, Aai's health improved over a period of time and I did not have to leave college before graduation.

When we thought that the swing of the pendulum of fortune had started moving towards 'good', we received one more blow. Tai was detected with Type 1 diabetes at the age of seventeen. Some related it to the stress and tension of mother's illness while some expressed their doubt that my father might have been diabetic. Whatever may be the reason but the fact was that she would be required to take insulin injection for life. Aai announced, "Since Nilima is diagnosed with diabetes and has been asked to avoid eating sweets, all of us should voluntarily give up eating the same, till she gets married and leaves our house." Except for morning tea, where sugar was used, mother neither made any sweets nor added sugar or jaggery in any vegetables or dal.

G S College was probably the only college in India which had a 'Students' Bank'. It used to accept deposits from students of the college for the purpose of lending to needy students. I became Secretary of the Bank for a two-year term. Although there was a Professor of our college to guide us, all the transactions were managed by a committee of students. The minimum amount required for opening an account was ₹5 and a loan of up to ₹500 was given to students at ten to twelve per cent per annum when Banks used to charge interest at eighteen to twenty per cent.

We used to give loan to students without asking for a guarantee or a collateral. The Bank which started at the initiative of Principal Tokhi turned out to be a boon to the students. Many students staying in hostels depended on money orders from their parents. Often they had some unexpected expenses or the money orders reached late, the bank used to come to their rescue for their short term needs. We used to have a 'verification check' of the reason mentioned in the application form for the loan. The entire amount collected by way of deposits and repayment of loans was used to disburse new loans. Hardly any balance remained by the tenth of every month in the Receipt and Payment Account. Maintaining ledgers of deposits and loans, applying monthly interest, documentation of loans, preparation of Trial Balance, making Profit & Loss Account and Balance Sheet was done only by the students. My active involvement in the Students' Bank helped me to become popular among the college students which ultimately resulted in getting me elected as a General Secretary of Students' Council for the year 1975-76.

During my college days, I was quite active in the Akhil Bharatiya Vidyarthi Parishad (ABVP). Incidentally Dattaji Didolkar who taught me Physics at JTC was the All India President. Although it was a student's organisation, it was always supported by teachers and professors who believed in ideals. I was its executive committee member representing G S College.

During the year 1975-76 when student council elections were held, I contested for the post of general secretary and got elected by a handsome margin. The next three months, till December 1975 were going to be quite hectic as we had to organise a gathering and prize distribution function thereafter for the winners of various competitions like drama, elocution, sports, debate etc. We had also decided to give lunch to all the students on the last day of the gathering. Tokhiji had magnanimously approved a budget of ₹25,000 for the students' union activities but had warned that the bills and vouchers should be properly accounted for and there should not be any extravagance. The entire executive council supported me to make the programmes successful.

The college gathering was an important event. There were some notorious students who took pleasure in passing loud comments during dramas or during a speech given by a dignitary. We decided to appoint well built 'Marshals' i.e. hefty students who would ensure that 'trouble makers' are removed from the *pandal* and are 'treated' well. Marshals were very useful in ensuring that no untoward incident happened in the gathering.

Principal of BYK College, Nashik, Dr M S Gosavi was invited to inaugurate the gathering. Professor Arwind alias Balluji Khandekar, our Marathi professor, helped me prepare my welcome speech. It covered the various activities the college undertook, including the students' bank and the morning prayer. G S College was probably the only college which had a morning prayer (like school) and many students and a few professors who had the first lecture would attend. (I was told that the practice of morning prayer continues in the college even now). Balluji added a few quotations by Sant Tukaram, Swami Vivekananda and Babasaheb Ambedkar in the speech and asked me to read them. The ten to fifteen minutes speech was well appreciated even by the chief guest, who started his speech with the quote of Swami Vivekananda I read at the end of my speech. "We want education by which character is formed, strength of mind is increased, the intellect is expanded and by which one can stand on one's own feet."

The second day was full of English/Hindi/Marathi dramas (one act plays), mimicry, and an orchestra and was thoroughly enjoyed by the students. The third day was the most challenging one as we had to arrange lunch for over a thousand students, professors and staff members. In order to save money, we decided that even though professional cooks would be engaged, all the material, utensils etc. would be arranged by the 'At home committee'. One of my friends suggested that Nitin Gadkari had a good number of big utensils at Gadkari Wada. He said that he would arrange the utensils. To our surprise, Nitin Gadkari himself came on a bullock cart and handed over all the utensils as per our need and his greatness was that he did not charge any rent for the same even though that year he was not a student at G S College. That showed his leadership qualities. He later became an acclaimed political leader and a Cabinet Minister. All the volunteers helped in serving lunch and everybody enjoyed the hot lunch served at the pandal. Proper planning and delegation of work to honest and responsible friends enabled us to celebrate the gathering without any hitch and all the expenses were well within the budget. It was a very big learning experience for me.

My mother played a great role in shaping my personality. Being a teacher, she used to tell us stories and incidents and then ask us to express our views. If our line of thinking was illogical or negative she would ask leading questions so that we could change our thought process. She always said that no job was insignificant. She said, "I won't mind, Nilesh, even if you decide to be a hairdresser, but those who visit your salon even once for a haircut, should say, "We won't go to any other hair cutting saloon as long as Nilesh is here!'." We must maintain dignity of labour.

After the half-yearly college exam for second year B.Com. was over, Aai enquired with me about my plan during the three weeks of Diwali vacation. I did not plan any specific activity but she had planned one for me. There was a famous cloth shop named Anjali on West High Court Road. It was always crowded. We used to buy our school uniform and clothes from the same shop. She said, "During Diwali the shop is always flooded with customers. I have spoken with the owner. From tomorrow for the next fifteen days you will go to the shop from five to eight-thirty in the evening to help him. Since you are a commerce student, you need to get practical experience of selling." I was also delighted to spend the evenings in the shop rather than whiling away my time in gossip and chit chat with friends. It was a good learning experience for me. I learnt to understand from the body language of a customer, whether he had come just to spend his time or was a genuine buyer or whether he would bargain. There were code words written on the chit tied to the cardboard over which the cloth was rolled. It indicated the least rate, below which the cloth should not be sold even if the customer bargained. The code number used to be alphanumeric and was written in such a way that even if the customer sees it, he won't understand it. For example, if the cloth is not to be sold below ₹42 per metre, the code would be D2. Similarly, for ₹36 it would be C6. Roughly twenty per cent above this rate was told to the customer first but it had to be ensured that the customer pays above the code number. Before leaving, I would have the entire cash counted, tied into bundles of hundred, fill up the paying in slips for cash and cheques. The owner often appreciated the speed at which I counted cash, filled up the paying slips etc.

At the end of my vacation, the owner asked me to take a shirt piece of my choice and said, "I appreciate your mother because she thought differently for you."

The B.Com. final year exams were generally held in the last week of March. I knew that three months of serious study would be enough for me to score good marks. Till the second fortnight of December 1975 time was spent on the Student Council elections, gatherings, ABVP activities, cricket etc. and less time was spent on studies. Still in the half yearly exams, I scored a first class. From the second or third week of December, I started studying for eight to ten hours a day. In the meanwhile I came across an advertisement for the recruitment of clerks in Canara Bank. Those in the final year of graduation were allowed to apply. Many students from my class applied for the job. The written test was held just before the B.Com. final exam. With my strong base in Maths, logic and reasonably good English, I found the exam quite easy. About a month after my B.Com. exams, I got a call for an interview. Only two or three of my friends from my class could clear the written test. I was interviewed in Nagpur and was quite sure of being selected.

As per the schedule, my B.Com. final exam was over in the first week of April 1976. The results were announced in the last week of May. I had missed first class by a whisker. I missed the first division by only one per cent! It was the shock of my life. There were only eight students that year that passed B.Com. in first class. Although I was in the top ten, as per the practice of the university, only those passing in first class were shown in the merit list. My heart sank but Aai said, "You spent more time in your extracurricular activities than necessary and you had to pay the price for the same. But there is no point in repenting. Perhaps your overall growth may help you build your career." Her words of solace comforted me but I ensured that I passed my M.Com. in first class with distinction just three years thereafter.

Soon after passing B.Com., I received a letter from Canara Bank about my selection and posting in the Foreign Exchange Department, International Division, Fort, Mumbai. I was the only one in the class to get selected and was probably the first to get a job in a bank. I decided to join Canara Bank. I was just nineteen then. I kept my mark lists, documents, appointment letter, clothes, some money in one suitcase and another handbag that had my night clothes, a book to read, a napkin, slippers etc. I left Nagpur by Dadar Express leaving at 10:10 pm. Many of my friends had come to the platform to wish me a happy journey. I introduced myself to my fellow passengers in the compartment. Notable among them was one Mr Venkateshwaran, who was a senior finance officer in a cotton mill in Chalisgaon. Before going to bed on the top berth I tied my suitcase with a chain to the hook below the lower berth but before doing so I took 'care' to put my watch, wallet and the ticket in the suitcase. Lights were switched off and I had such a sound sleep that I woke up only when I heard that the train had stopped in the morning at Bhusawal station. I got down to brush my teeth and to have a hot cup of tea. I was shocked to find that in the night my suitcase along with the chain and lock was stolen. In the meanwhile I heard another passenger shouting loudly that his suitcase was also stolen. I enquired with the fellow passengers but they had no idea. I met the TC on the platform and told him that I wanted to file a Police complaint. He dissuaded me from doing so saying,

"You have already lost the suitcase, you will miss the train if you want to go to the station master." Mr Venkateswaran comforted me by offering me a cup of tea and the train left the station. A new team of ticket checkers boarded the train from Bhusawal. A TC came to check my ticket. I had foolishly kept my ticket in the suitcase which was stolen. But Mr Venkateshwaran came to my rescue. He told the TC about the theft and also confirmed that my ticket was checked by the TC from Nagpur. He also requested him to ensure my safe exit from Dadar station.

I was dumbfounded. No money, no appointment letter, no ticket, no certificates. I was controlling my tears when Mr Venkateshwaran took out ₹100 from his pocket and gave it to me. When my salary was ₹430 per month, ₹100 meant a lot in those days. He consoled me and said, "I will get down at Chalisgaon. Don't be in a hurry to return my money. Do so when you get your first salary or even later when you have enough savings." He gave me his visiting card and got down. I sent him his money by money order two months later. The TC ensured that I had a safe exit at Dadar station. I went to one of our relatives in Dadar who helped me in getting new sets of clothes. The next day I went to Canara Bank and met the concerned officer who confirmed my credentials from my application form for employment which had my photograph. He advised me to write an application stating that the original certificates were lost and the duplicate ones would be submitted within the next two months. He then issued me an Order asking me to join Foreign Exchange Dept., Fort, Mumbai. My service in Canara Bank began from the next day. I stayed in Dadar as a paying guest. During that period, I cleared two groups of Inter ICWAI and passed the prelims of the Indian Civil Services (IAS), I did not, somehow, pursue increasing my educational qualification beyond M.Com. and CAIIB. All other courses, I left midway. But my score of ninety-five out of a hundred in Maths in ICWAI was probably the highest in the subject that year. I could, later, pass M.Com. in first class which I had marginally missed in B.Com.

Before joining Canara Bank, I had appeared for the written test for the post of clerk cum cashier in Bank of India. I was called for an interview and in April 1977 I got an appointment from Bank of India with my first posting in Sitabuldi Branch, Nagpur. I resigned from Canara Bank after working there for eight to nine months to join Bank of India. I was happy that I could come back to Nagpur and stay with Aai.

My appointment letter from Bank of India mentioned that I was appointed under the 'Branch Expansion Programme' and my first posting after initial training in Sitabuldi Branch would be as a clerk cum cashier at some other Branch which would be made known later. I joined Sitabuldi Branch where Mr P P Agarwal was the Agent. (In those days, the Branch head was designated as Agent). On my first day, after introducing me to other staff members and officers, he called for two packets of hundred notes of ₹10 and demonstrated how notes should be counted. He said, "Put the left palm edge with a little pressure on the lower part of the note to ensure that eighty per cent of the notes are visible. Count notes with their face down as the torn notes pasted from behind can be checked. Don't make haste. If cash is short, it is the cashier's responsibility. Don't talk to anybody while counting notes as you may forget the count. If the packet is of less or more notes than hundred, count again. While counting, do not look here and there. Pay full attention to the notes you are counting." He also showed me a few 'two piece notes' and fake notes which were not accepted by RBI and said, "If you accept such notes by mistake, it's your loss..." There was no note counting machine in those days. These inputs were invaluable. I was also trained on various counters of the bank like savings bank, current deposits, cash credit, loans and advances, bills for collection, debit notes/ credit notes, demand drafts, despatch etc. I was also trained on how to calculate interest, make daily summary of transactions, how to prepare a 'Friday Statement' etc. I took keen interest in learning all the jobs. Mr Agarwal was a very active officer. I never saw him sitting idle in his cabin. During staff shortage, he would even come out to post cheques in the ledger. He made an indelible impression on my mind. My stay in the Branch came to an end after seven months when I was issued an office order in November 1977 transferring me to Lakhandur Branch, District Bhandara, which was to be opened soon. I was happy to go there for two reasons, one that initially since there won't be much work, I would be able to study and the second, I would get 'signing authority' and cashier's allowance which was almost twenty per cent of my salary.

The next day, I left Nagpur by Nagpur-Lakhandur bus via Sakoli leaving at 7:00 am. I reached Lakhandur at about 11:30 am. From Sakoli onwards, there was a metal road. A lot of dust had settled on my clothes and I must have inhaled a good amount of dust on way to reaching Lakhandur. The Branch was at walking distance from the bus station. It was probably the only building in Lakhandur which was a concrete two storey building. I met the Agent, Mr Girish U Trivedi. He was posted from Mumbai. He told me that it was for the first time in his life that he left Mumbai and had never stayed in a village. That way I was well conversant with rural life as I had spent three years of my childhood in villages which were even smaller than Lakhandur. The next day was the day of the Branch inauguration. Carpentry work was on going. A big Godrej safe for keeping cash arrived. I salute the workers who managed to lift it and put it on an iron bracket. It was so heavy that if by chance it fell on anyone, the person would be crushed under its weight. We moved around distributing invitation cards. The entrance was decorated. Bhandara Main Branch helped us in making flower arrangements, decorations, sweets, printing of invitation cards etc.

Lakhandur was a village with a population of about five thousand. It had a Zilla Parishad School up to SSC, a Co-operative Bank, Primary Health Centre (PHC) and a Block Development Office (BDO). But it had no lodge or a hotel. We had no choice but to stay in the Branch office itself, though it was not advisable.

The inauguration ceremony was attended by the sitting MLA, Mr Hiralalji Bhaiyya who was a wholesale paddy merchant. He along with Mr D K Khopkar, Area Manager, Bank of India cut the ribbon. A large number of merchants, traders, farmers, Government officials from PHC and BDO had assembled. Ninety-two savings/current accounts were opened and cash of over ₹1600 was collected on the first day. It was a modest collection for the opening day.

The Branch Manager's residence which was on the first floor of the Bank building was in the finishing stages. We stayed in the Branch for a week. On the third day another staff, agricultural clerk Subhash Bhendarkar joined. We searched for a house and shifted to a four room block in Parshuram Patil's *chawl*. It had eight such blocks and four toilet blocks, while the bathroom was attached. The monthly rent was ₹50. (My salary at the time was ₹450 per month!) While we were staying in the Branch, Hiralalji Bhaiyya, who had a house just opposite to our Branch, offered us accommodation and food which was politely denied by Mr Trivedi. When I asked him why, he said, "Nilesh, he is rich, he is influential. If we accept his favour, in the future if he asks for a favour from us, it would be difficult for us to decline." Although such a situation did not arise, but not accepting favour from clients was the first lesson taught by Mr Trivedi.

The next Sunday, I went to Nagpur and I brought my bicycle, a few utensils, crockery, a stove etc. We engaged a cook although I had a liking for cooking. Within a month we settled down in Lakhandur.

Lakhandur was situated on the banks of river Chulbandh, which was a tributary of Vainganga. I never saw the river becoming a riverlet. It always flowed fuller with good speed. The fields were always green with paddy crops. Soil was fertile and due to canal irrigation, farmers used to reap three crops a year. People were rich but lacked banking habits.

I was getting enough time to study in the bank as well as at home. During the first year at Lakhandur, I appeared for Civil Services and passed the prelims but the main exam was too tough for me. I appeared for M.Com. Part I and secured the second position in order of merit. I passed the first banking exam called Certified Associate of Indian Institute of Bankers (C.A.I.I.B.). The next year, I passed the M.Com. examination in the first division. I was determined to secure the first division in M.Com. as I was not happy with myself for missing the first division in the B.Com. examination, though by a whisker. I also passed the Hindi exam. '*Kovid*' which was equivalent to graduation in Hindi. The bank used to encourage its employees to appear for Hindi exams and used to pay an incentive of ₹100 on passing the exams.

It was difficult for us to popularise 'banking' in and around Lakhandur as farmers were used to dealing in cash or credit from lenders. But when they realized that the rates of interest charged by our bank on farm loan, equipment loan, more suited to their pocket, they started transacting with the bank. We disbursed quite a few tractor loans. On some days, there would not be a single transaction. On such days, before the close of cash hours, Mr Trivedi, the Agent would withdraw ₹50 in cash from his account and deposit it in my account and I used to withdraw from my account and deposit the same amount in his account. This was necessary to dispel doubts in the minds of 'higher ups' that the Branch was closed on that day. In the second and subsequent years such situations did not arise. During crop loan disbursal days, the Branch used to be quite crowded. Same was the case on weekly bazaar days.

A cashier needs to be ever alert. A slight slip of attention may lead to heavy financial loss. A person who has worked as a cashier knows the great satisfaction he gets, once the 'Receipt minus Payment equal to Balance' equation tallies at the end of the day. I have not come across any bank cashier who has never accepted a two piece note, and/or a fraudulent note by mistake or did not have short/excess cash any time in his career. One day an illiterate farmer came to withdraw a small amount from his bank account. My friend Subhash Bhendarkar helped him fill up the withdrawal slip, took his thumb impression on the same and it came to me duly approved for payment through the officer. I gave him the amount without collecting the slip which I had given to him to put his thumb impression. Before leaving the bank, he looked perplexed. The sub staff asked him if the cash was correct. He questioned, "What do I have to do with this pink slip?" (Withdrawal slips were pink in colour.) The sub staff took it from the farmer and gave it to me which made me realise my mistake. Of course, I had to offer tea to all staff members as a penalty, as was the tradition prevalent then. I was obviously saved from a shortage of cash to the extent of the amount on that withdrawal slip. It could have been traced but getting hold of the withdrawal slip carried by the farmer would have been a herculean task.

But one day when I found my cash short by ₹4,000, it made me sweat. If the cash was not recovered, in order to tally the cash book at the end of the day, I would have to shell out seven to eight months' salary.

It was a Tuesday which was the weekly bazaar day. We had also announced disbursement of crop loans that day. The loanee farmers were waiting outside the Branch to get loans even before the Branch opened for the day. I started my work at 11:00 am sharp. (Cash timing was from 11:00 am to 3:00 pm) The Branch was unusually crowded that day. At the end of cash hours, there were still some disbursements pending. As the farmers had come from far off places, it would be inconsiderate to send them back. I closed the cash counter at almost 4:00 pm. We had a cup of tea and I started 'balancing the cash'. Over one hundred and fifty transactions had occurred that day. I found that the cash in my box had a shortfall of ₹4,000. I checked all the vouchers of receipts and payments again, totalled the payment book and receipt book but the shortfall could not be located. Subhash Bhendarkar came to help me to recount the cash. Finally, I told Mr Prakash Naik, the Manager (By then the designation of Agent was changed to Manager) that there appeared to be a shortage in cash to the extent of ₹4,000. He was also exhausted with the heavy work that day. He said, "I will have a smoke outside, drink a cup of hot tea and return in ten minutes. Till then if you are not able to trace the shortfall I will come to check where the mistake is." We checked everything again but to no avail. I was becoming desperate.

That day, a thought came to my mind. I asked myself, "Why am I doing this risky job? Today if this ₹4,000 shortage is to be made good by me, it will be equal to my seven to eight months' salary." I was sweating. In the meanwhile, Mr Naik came and asked for all the vouchers of receipts and payments. Mostly there were withdrawal slips and a few cheques. He was minutely going through each voucher, checking if the denominations written on the back side of the voucher, matched with the amount written on withdrawal slip or cheque. Suddenly he called me and showed me the withdrawal slip of Hiralalji Bhaiyya. He said, "Nilesh, most probably you have paid ₹18,000 to Hiralalji instead of ₹14,000. Looking at the withdrawal slip, even my first impression was that the amount in figures was ₹18,000." The '4' in Marathi (Devanagari) was written in such a way that it looked like '8' in English. I locked the cashier's cabin and rushed to his house which was just opposite our Branch.

I saw him and heaved a sigh of relief. I said, "*Shethji* you had come to withdraw cash today. I doubt if I have paid you the correct amount. Will you please check, I am short of ₹4,000 today." He gave me the cotton bag which he had tucked below his *gaddi* (seat) and said, "I have not even counted it. You count it and if there is excess, you take it." I took out the cash, counted it and found it to be ₹18,000. In order to confirm again, I asked him, "*Shethji*, how much did you withdraw today?" He promptly said ₹14,000. Mystery was solved. I told him, "The cash here is ₹18,000. It appears that I paid you ₹4,000 in excess. You may count it if you wish." He said, "Satheji I am sorry. I should have counted the cash before leaving the Branch. Had I done so, your running around could have been avoided. Please excuse me and take the excess cash of ₹4,000."

I took the cash, thanked him and came running to the Branch. Looking at my smiling face, both my colleagues who were equally anxious understood what the smile meant. I added that money to the cash on hand and tallied the cash. When Mr Naik came to the cash cabin to sign the daily cash balance book, he said in a humorous way, "Nilesh the hair on my head is turning grey not by standing in sunlight, it is due to the experiences that I have gained by working in the bank." We laughed together.

And mind you, Mr Hiralalji Bhaiyya was the sitting MLA. What a modesty! What a simplicity! My salute!

One evening, I received a surprise visit from Aai. She came from Nagpur without any intimation. I was at home and on hearing a knock at the door, I opened it to find her standing at the door. I was very happy to see her but equally surprised. My friend Subhash Bhendarkar said, "*Maoshi* (aunty) has paid us a surprise visit to check on us and see whether we are indulging in drinking, betting, playing cards etc." The smile on her face was an indication that the purpose of her surprise visit was none other than the one mentioned by Subhash. We had a hearty laugh. We enjoyed the food cooked by her for the next two days, before she left. She did not have to come to Lakhandur on a 'surprise check' again since soon thereafter I got transferred to Mahal Branch, Nagpur. When my substitute joined, I left Lakhandur with an enriching experience of four years and a couple of degrees under the belt.

I joined Mahal Branch, Nagpur when I was almost twenty-five years old, which was considered a marriageable age then. One day my mother asked me about my intent and plans. I told her in clear terms that I would soon become an officer in Bank of India. She probably heaved a sigh of relief but then very cleverly said, "In that case, I wish that you get married first before becoming an officer. I know that the officers are initially posted in far off Branches, then it will be difficult for me to find an alliance for you. So long as you are in Nagpur, I want you to get married." She was right and there was no reason for me to say 'No'. She soon spread the word through her acquaintances and friends that proposals of marriageable girls from Nagpur may be sent to her since I had decided to marry. Accordingly, she received a proposal of Mr Balwant Sane's daughter from one of her acquaintances. We visited their house in Laxmi Nagar in the traditional way of meeting the girl, Ms Mrunalini, whom I liked in the first meeting itself. We were married on 21 March 1982 and Ms Mrunalini Sane, an Assistant in LIC of India, Amravati Branch, became Mrs Nilambari Sathe. Soon she got transferred to the Nagpur Divisional office and a new phase in my life began.

Lessons Learnt...

- Proper planning and delegation helps in execution of work.
- We must maintain dignity of labour.
- Never accept favours from Bank customers.
- While at work, do it with full concentration.

III

Initial Grooming in LIC

One day, maybe in August or so, Nilambari came home to show me an advertisement for the post of Assistant Administrative Officers (AAO) to be recruited by LIC. The last date for submission through the proper channel was just two days away. I went through the advertisement but told her that I would soon become Officer in the bank and had no inclination to join LIC. She was smart in saying, "Nobody has offered you the post. There are only sixty vacancies. It's an all India selection. There is a written test followed by an interview. To join or not will be decided only when you get selected. Prove yourself by at least passing the written test." The last sentence was quite challenging. I decided to apply and show her that I was intelligent enough to clear the written test. I applied and started preparation for the written test. After the exam was over, I was confident of getting a call for an interview as I got everything right in my Maths and English objective papers and did reasonably well in G.K. As expected I was called for the interview in Mumbai. I learnt that there were five from the Nagpur centre out of three hundred and twenty candidates from all over India who were called for an interview.

I was not worried about the interview as I was good at English, my understanding of socio-economic-political issues was good and I had no stage fear. I was interviewed for about twenty-five minutes. Mr J Mathan, retired Chairman of LIC along with three others asked me a variety of questions on poverty, caste system, population problem, economic issues faced by India, pluses and minuses of dams like Bhakra-Nangal. From the facial expressions of the interviewers I could guess that I had done well in the interview. Finally, one member asked, "Why do you want to leave a bank to join LIC when you are likely to become an officer there?" To this I gave an honest reply, "Since my wife is in LIC, and LIC has a policy to post husband and wife in the same place, it may help us to lead a better family life." To this, the committee members laughed and wished me 'best of luck'. Although I was sure of getting selected, I did not underestimate the other candidates' wisdom. But I was satisfied with my interview. In the first week of April 1983 I received a telegram from LIC that I was selected as AAO and I was asked to join Officers' Training College (OTC), Borivali, Mumbai within a week's time. When Nilambari shared this news with her boss at LIC, he said, "Do you know that although LIC had announced sixty vacancies of AAOs, only forty to forty-five of the most deserving candidates have been selected and your husband is one of them." She probably realised that her choice of selecting me as a life partner was not wrong!

I was also happy but I was finding it difficult to leave Nilambari alone when she was seven months pregnant. But there was no choice. It was the beginning of a new life.

I resigned from Bank of India and joined OTC as an Apprentice Officer. I had never stayed in a hostel during my college days. When I reached the hostel, many officers had already arrived. There were nearly forty of us and were allotted rooms on a twin sharing basis. The officers were from various states like Uttar Pradesh, Bihar, Odisha, Madhya Pradesh, Andhra Pradesh, Tamil Nadu, Kerala, Karnataka, Delhi, Maharashtra etc. Out of the forty-two officers who joined on the first day in OTC, there were two Marathi speaking officers, Sarojini Dikhale from Mumbai and me from Nagpur.

The next day, we were instructed to assemble at 9:00 am in the training college which was in the adjoining building. A typical English breakfast of cornflakes, omelette, toast, tea, coffee and fruits was ready at 7:30 am. We were quite particular about being ready to reach the college assembly hall five minutes before 9:00 am. The first session was chaired by the Principal where the entire faculty was seated behind us. He introduced all of them and then we introduced ourselves. It was great fun to restart college again after seven years. The time-table indicated seven daily lectures from Monday to Friday and four lectures on Saturday on various topics. The first day was over. I had taken down notes of what was taught. I revised those before going to bed. It helped because the next day, at 9:00 am when we had assembled in the class room the Principal said, "I forgot to tell you that daily one of you will have to come to the dais and briefly explain what was taught yesterday. All the professors will be present and may ask clarification to assess if the subject was properly understood. Even if it was not informed well in advance, is there anyone who will voluntarily come to the dais and review the subjects taught yesterday?"

There was pin drop silence. He again asked, "If no one is ready, I have got your names written on pieces of paper and kept in this box. I will pick up a chit and the student, whose name is found there, will have to present a review." Since I had taken proper notes and had revised before coming to class, I raised my hand. The Principal was happy. I covered the topics in ten minutes then a few professors asked for some clarification which I gave and the other students heaved a sigh of relief as they were saved.

The next day onwards, taking out a slip from the box and a review by that student was regularly followed. The timetable was drawn in such a way that we were supposed to know the subjects like policy conditions, accounts, actuarial science, IT, staff regulations, disciplinary proceedings, marketing of insurance etc. which were covered at length.

We were mostly of the same age. Nearly one-third were younger than me. A few of us, including me, were married but without exception all of us were enthusiastic and depending on their common liking, formed groups...birds of the same feather - smokers, boozers, studious, sportsmen etc. There were twelve girls and thirty boys.

During those days when cell phones were unheard of, there was one common 'paid' phone in the canteen. We were allowed to make calls and receive calls as well. On the evening of 13 June 1983 I received a phone call from Nagpur informing me that Nilambari had delivered a baby boy. I had become a father. It was a matter of celebration. After dinner, I invited all my friends to the sweetmeat shop which was near our hostel and treated them with Amul *shrikhand*. I was surprised to find that many of my friends from the North had not tasted *shrikhand* in the past. One of my dear friends, Vinay Sah remembers it even today that he tasted *shrikhand* for the first time in his life when my son Himanshu was born.

There was a coloured TV in the canteen. Most of us were cricket lovers. World Cup matches were on in England and we used to be glued to the screen after dinner. The climax was reached on 25 June 1983 when the final match between India and West Indies was played. It was after midnight when we won the exciting match. We were so excited that we started beating the tables, dancing and rejoicing aloud without understanding that in the adjoining area were the quarters of professors and our shouting would disturb them. We realised it only the next day when after the routine review session, Principal Mr S M Shirodkar expressed his unhappiness over our unruly behaviour at midnight, which disturbed the sleep of the professors and their family members, who had complained to him about the same. Our heads hung down in shame when we heard his last sentence, "Your unruly behaviour was not only unbecoming of a responsible officer of LIC but also as a civilized citizen." After such a heavy dose of wisdom that was given to us, the other professors left the class and Mr Shirodkar continued his lecture on marketing. We saw a different Shirodkar when just before leaving the classroom, he said, "Well, I scolded you in the capacity of a Principal. But don't take it to heart. I also watched the match and had I been of your age, I would have also celebrated the victory the same way. Be yourself." This comment released our tension and we had smiles on our faces.

We were quite serious about our studies for the seven months of training. We were asked our choice of posting fifteen days before the end of our training. We expected our choice would be given consideration, but to our dismay, except Sarojini Dikhale, all of us were posted at far off places from our postings of choice. A day before the postings were announced, we had a gathering where I sang two songs. There was a skit, mimicry, *qawwali* etc. This joy lasted only for a day. Tickets were handed over to us the next day and we had to leave within the next forty-eight hours. We had a great bonding in those seven months of togetherness and many were in tears while leaving the O.T.C. I too left for Satara and then to join the Sangli Branch as A.A.O., leaving behind, the enjoyment with friends and the greenery of O.T.C.

I arrived in Sangli where initially, for a week or ten days, I stayed in a guest house which was in the Branch premises. Mr Bapusaheb Lawte was the Branch Manager who helped me find accommodation. We finalised a three room house owned by Mrs Yadao in Shivaji Nagar with a rent of ₹470 per month and a deposit of ₹1500. Nilambari was in Nagpur. She applied for a request transfer to Sangli and in a couple of months her transfer was in effect. I went to Nagpur to shift my family in January 1984 and soon thereafter, our routine started. Nilambari joined the Policy Servicing department while I was in charge of Finance and Accounts. Owing to my earlier banking experience, I found my assignment easy but quite interesting.

Those days, salaries were paid in cash. Based on the net payment of salary to each employee, I worked out the denomination wise cash that was required for disbursement, withdrew it from the bank, made salary envelopes, wrote names of the respective employees and they would come to me, sign across the revenue stamp on the salary sheet and take the envelope. It was quite smooth. After some time, Mr Shantinath Hukkeri, an Assistant, about fifty years old, came to me and said, "Sir, will you please write my name on another envelope and write ₹530 on it?" (His actual take home salary was ₹940 or so.) I did so but I asked him the reason. He said, "Sir, I handover only basic pay to my wife and with the balance I buy NSCs every month." I was taken aback. I learnt the first lesson in savings and investment. Saving is not what remains at the end of the month but what you wilfully set aside at the beginning of the month and manage your expenses with the balance left.

Sangli district being on the border of Karnataka, many employees used to speak in Kannada, even though they were Maharashtrians. It amused me. We had a Development Officer named Mr B B Inamdar. He was good in Marathi and used to quote Sanskrit *shlokas* quite often. He was staying in *Brahman Ali* (lane) in Miraj. It took me five to six months to know that he was a Muslim. It was only when one day Balasaheb Khandekar, an Assistant called him by his full name when a phone call had come for him, "There is a phone call for you, Mr Bilal Badshah Inamdar." I asked him one day how he is so good in Marathi. He said, "Mr Sathe, I have done my masters in Marathi and Sanskrit. All members of my family fast on chaturthi as lord Ganesh is the *Gram Daivat* (Deity of the town). I stay in Brahman Ali, where most families are Brahmins. We do get the smell of chicken, mutton, fish being cooked in our neighbours' houses but we do not even eat an egg." It was a great revelation for me.

On one Sunday, I accompanied Bapusaheb Lawte, our Branch Manager, to a village near Kavathe Mahankal, a tehsil in Sangli district, known for drought and famine. The road after Miraj was dusty. We went there by his Premier Padmini car. Owning such a car was a matter of prestige in those days. An Agent who wanted help from Bapusaheb in closing the insurance sale accompanied us in the car. 'Closing' is always considered the most difficult part in the insurance sales process. After travelling for about an hour and a half and covering a distance of about fifty kilometres, we reached the residence of the client which was almost in the midst of his agricultural land. Many children in the adjoining houses came near the car as it was a rare experience and a novelty for them, as they had to walk for ten kilometres to avail the bus service.

We were greeted with respect. As per tradition we were offered a piece of jaggery with water. The mud house was in good condition with a straw-stacked roof. The only chair was offered to Bapusaheb while we sat on the wooden cot called *khat* or *khatiya.* After exchanging pleasantries, the Agent introduced the host as his brother-in-law and a respectable person in the vicinity being the only person who studied up to matriculation from that area (called *panchkroshi*). Bapusaheb thereafter took the reins and said, "You need to have a policy of ₹3 lakh." To which the client was repeatedly talking about drought, famine etc. and finally said, "I won't be able to afford beyond ₹1 lakh." While tea was being served, he went in the house and came out with ten bundles of ₹100 each. I was wonderstruck to see the poor farmer with ₹1 lakh cash. Bapusaheb started laughing. He said, "I know you can afford to have a policy of ₹3 lakh which we will now close. I do not want ₹1 lakh from you but want only ₹20,000 as the policy premium. The balance may be taken back. I am giving you a 15 year policy for which you will pay ₹20,000 per annum and you will get more than ₹5 lakh at the end of the term which will come handy for the wedding of your daughter who is three years old now." I do not know how much of that was understood by the client, but he was happy to take back ₹80,000 which was clear from his smiling face. This was my first field experience of selling insurance which I thoroughly enjoyed. The Agent was very happy since it was a big sale for him.

Sometimes in order to clear pending work, I used to go to the office even on Sundays. On one such Sunday while returning from office, I met with an accident. I was on my motorcycle driving in the right direction on a one-way road while suddenly an Ambassador car came out of a lane and took a wrong turn hitting my motorcycle. I fell off the bike to notice that my left hand above the wrist was dangling. I went to a nearby hospital and called my friend, Dr Ashok Deshpande, Anesthesiologist, who stayed near my house. He took me home on his scooter. He asked me when the surgery should be done. I said, as early as possible.

He contacted Dr Arwade, an Orthopaedic Surgeon and asked me to get admitted the next day by 7:00 am. Surgery was scheduled for 8:30 am.

To our surprise at around 10:00 pm, Ashok came to our house and said, "Tomorrow being a new moon day (considered 'unauspicious'), already four surgeries scheduled for the next day have been cancelled by other patients. Dr Arwade wants our confirmation." I said, "Ashok, the accident happened on a day which was not considered as unauspicious. Why should the surgery not be done on the so-called unauspicious day?" I never believed in such superstitions. Nilambari endorsed my view. She said, "Moreover since it will be the only surgery, the surgeon will not be in a hurry and he will do his job better." Ashok left and as decided we went to hospital the next day and I got admitted for surgery at 7:00 am with an empty stomach.

Dr Ashok and my other friend Dr Vikas Kurhekar gave me anaesthesia and to their surprise my skin became full red. The drug pethidine used in anaesthesia did not suit me. They soon gave me an antidote and it took me some time to stabilize. Nilambari got worried as she was told that I would be out of O. T. in an hour but it took me over two and half hours to be out. Ashok informed her later about the allergy and she had a smile on her face when jokingly he said, "*Vahini*, after many years when Nilesh will become Chairman of LIC, I will tell everyone that I had made him unconscious!" I got discharged the next day and came home with a plaster from my bicep to wrist. Nilambari informed Sudhir, Tai's husband, who had by then become a Senior Sub-Editor in Tarun Bharat newspaper in Nagpur, about the fracture and operation requesting him to inform Aai. How could Aai wait at Nagpur when her beloved son met with an accident? Immediately Sudhir and Aai reached Sangli by train.

My plaster was removed after three weeks. After a week thereafter, I was transferred to Kolhapur on job rotation from the administrative wing to the marketing wing. Only seven AAOs in the entire Western Zone were posted on marketing side. I was one of them. I joined 947 Branch, Kolhapur. As I had a marketing role, I was now eligible for a car and a residential telephone which was considered to be prestigious those days. Thus I got my first car at the age of twenty-nine. However we shall never forget Sangli as we were blessed with our second son, Kaustubh during our stay there.

Since Sangli and Kolhapur were under the same division (Satara, those days), Nilambari's transfer was not a problem. After my joining Kolhapur, she requested for a transfer which was approved within a week. She was posted in 949 Br. We rented a four room house on the ground floor, on Kalamba Road. Opposite to the house was a school named Tapovan which was a Marathi medium school (vernacular). Himanshu started attending this school in *Balak Mandir* (KG). Although I was a firm believer that education upto Class V should necessarily be given in Marathi, a senior officer from Satara, Mr Vishwas Dandekar, advised me to shift him to an English medium school as our jobs were transferable and as per the LIC policy on HR matters prevailing then, I was likely to be transferred to at least two other zones. As per his advice, we shifted him to Gokhale Education Society's English medium school the next year.

I involved myself in my work. My job was to help Agents and Development Officers (DOs) bring more and more new business premium and policies. I had seen how Mr. Bapusaheb Lawte used to help and support them. Here the Senior Branch Manager was Mr Balasaheb Gawde, who was another stalwart insurance marketeer. I started wearing a tie in order to impress the prospects. I studied features of all the plans of insurance that were compiled in a book called Agents' Manual. I used to go on a joint call (canvassing prospects) with Agents/D.Os. I was young and enthusiastic. I was quite friendly with the field force. That year, for the first time in the past three years, our Branch achieved its budget on new business premium and policies. I gained confidence that I would do well on the marketing side. I understood the pulse of field force. Help them, pat them, spare time for them, spend time with them, give them new ideas, help them to the extent you can and they will give their life for you. I did not need their life, what I needed was just more premium and more policies.

We had an LIC scheme where the premium was deducted from the insured person's salary. It was called the Salary Saving Scheme. It helped employees keep their policies in force as they would receive their monthly salary only after premium deduction. It was the best way to save as well. We had such a scheme in the office of Superintendent of Police (SP). I observed that there was no growth in monthly premium from the Police Department. There were a few Agents who were having more than a hundred policies under their agency from the SP office. I called them and asked the reason why they have stopped selling policies to the Police. The reason given was shocking. The Admin. persons in the SP's office responsible for disbursement of salaries of Police personnel, used to deduct the premium from their salary every month but would not pay it to LIC for ten to fifteen employees each month resulting in a 'gap' in premium. It was clear that these amounts were siphoned off. Obviously on these policies, the Agents were not getting commission hence they had stopped selling policies to Policemen. I checked the facts with Mr Nandkumar Jadhav, Higher Grade Assistant (HGA), who confirmed this. I went to S. P. Kolhapur's office one day along with Mr Jadhav, met the concerned person in the salary section and showed him the irregularity, to which the person arrogantly said, "Has anyone complained to you? These Policemen stand at traffic signals collecting bribe money but we are denied a penny. We are dying working in the office. For this reason, every month we deduct but don't remit the premium amount to LIC of a few Policemen. Do what you want to do." Mr Jadhav said, "Sir, I had told you that they are incorrigible. Let us go now." I said, "No, we will meet the S.P." We went to his PA, gave him my visiting card. The S.P. was a young IPS officer, almost my age. He called us in after sometime. I said, "Sir, we have introduced the salary saving scheme for the benefit of Policemen but this is what we have observed. Policemen are subject to a greater risk on life and have many vices like tobacco etc. We have recently settled a death claim of a thirty-five year old Policeman. But if your department does not remit the premium even if it is deducted, the policy will lapse and in case such a Policeman dies, LIC won't be able to pay anything to the bereaved family." I also narrated to him what the Policemen in the salary section had said. He listened to me carefully. He seemed to have understood the gravity of the subject. He promised us that he would look into the matter and we left. Mr Jadhav of course was sure that nothing would happen.

To our surprise, the next day, the same arrogant Policeman from the salary section came to our office to meet Mr Jadhav and said, "Please calculate and let me know the default amount. Sir has ordered me not to come back to office without reconciling the amount of premium deducted and amount remitted to LIC with respect to all Policemen for the last five years. I have brought pay sheets for the past five years." Mr Jadhav was taken aback. It took them almost fifteen days to get the reconciliation done and the fellow deposited the outstanding amount in cash at the counter, which in those days was quite huge (running in over a lakh of rupees). Thereafter every month remittance from S.P.'s office started coming regularly and duly reconciled with schedule. Agents became active and new policies of Policemen started pouring in.

Insurance sales depend on how many persons are in your contact list. We used to ask the newly appointed Agents to always keep adding new names in the prospects list. I advised the DOs to keep recruiting Agents from all castes, creeds and religions since it is easy to sell insurance to known persons and relatives rather than to the unknowns. I had observed that we did not have a single DO who was a Muslim, as a result of which we had almost no Agents who followed the Muslim faith. I had also noticed that although Kolhapur had a good number of Muslims staying there, we hardly used to get proposals from Muslims. I, therefore, was urging the DOs to recruit Muslim LIC Agents. Finally a graduate who was young and smart, Mr Mujawar was recruited by a DO as his Agent. In the first month itself he got six policies but thereafter I saw him only after three or four months. I asked him about how the business was going. He said, "Sir, I started with great enthusiasm and got six to eight policies. I noticed that there were not many Agents from our community hence was sure to do a good amount of business but my initial enthusiasm died down soon as many said that buying Insurance was against our religion. I could not convince them about how insurance would help them in achieving financial goals and I may have to give up my agency." I said, "Mujawar, don't get discouraged. Take an appointment with one of your prospects. I will come with you. Let us see if we can close a sale." He was happy. After two to three days, he came to office at closing hour and said, "Sir, my school teacher Mr Bagwan has agreed to meet us at 6:30 pm today." Since his DO had already left office, we decided to go without him.

We reached Mr Bagwan's house which gave me an impression that his earning may not be much but he welcomed us with warmth and praised Mr Mujawar as one of the best students in his class. As tea was being served, I enquired about Mr Bagwan's family. He had two sons, a wife and an old father. I told him that his student had taken the LIC Agency and requested him to help Mujawar in getting policies. He immediately said, "Sir, Muslims don't take insurance as it is considered Haram (against religion)." I explained to him, "Sir, insurance is the concept of spreading risk. It doesn't pay any interest (*'sood'* which is prohibited according to the Holy Quran). I will give you in writing that the policy does not pay any interest. The concept of insurance is similar to sharing a *roti* by many in a plate..." He seemed to be happy with my argument.

I then asked him, could he take his father for the Hajj pilgrimage since every Muslim has an ardent desire to go to Hajj at least once in his lifetime to which he replied, "Sir, it needs at least fifteen to twenty thousand rupees to go to Hajj. I could not save enough." I took a cue from his statement and said, "Sir, although your father could not go to Hajj, I assure you that you will go to Hajj." Now he became more alert. He asked me, "How?" I said, "Sir, you have two sons. How much do you spend on them monthly?" He said, "About hundred rupees each." I said, "Sir, consider an insurance policy as your third son. I am not sure if your two sons would be able to take you to Hajj. But I assure you that this third son will certainly take you to Hajj." His smile was a mark of his acceptance. I gave him a small endowment policy of ₹18,000 sum assured for fifteen years with a premium of about ₹100 per month and told him that he would get about ₹35,000 on maturity which would be enough for him to go to Hajj. He not only signed the proposal form but helped Mujawar sell fourteen policies to other school teachers. That month Mujawar was among the top Agents of the Branch. Thereafter he never looked back and became a successful LIC Agent.

I had forgotten this but one day in 2003-04, when I was Sr. Divisional Manager, Mumbai Division 1, my P. A. informed me that one Mr Bagwan was waiting to see me. I let him in. On seeing me, he said, "Sir, you might have forgotten me but I will never forget you. I am Bagwan, a teacher from Kolhapur whom you had given a policy calling it as my third son who would certainly take me to Hajj. And tonight, I am actually flying to Mecca. I have come to thank you for your advice. The policy matured giving me enough money for the Hajj pilgrimage," and he touched my feet seeking my blessings. It was an awkward moment for me. I said, "Bagwan sir, you are elder than me, please don't do so." To which he said, "I am getting blessings of Allah only due to you." I still remember his face glowing with a sense of fulfilment.

It was unusual to achieve business targets for two consecutive financial years. But Branch 947 did it. But before that, one day in March 1990, I got a firing from my boss, Babasaheb and the reason was quite funny.

I was so involved in field activities that consecutively for four or five days, I went on joint calls with Agents which used to end with the famous white mutton curry and *bhakri*. I would reach back home, not before 10:00 pm. One day on reaching home from office, when Nilambari noticed that I was not going to have dinner with her at home, she called Babasaheb and said, "Sir, when you meet Mr Sathe tomorrow in office, please tell him that I have invited him for dinner." He understood what she meant and next day said, "Nilesh, your children wait for you at dinner time. Business will happen but taking care of your family is also equally important. I do not want a similar complaint from Mrs Sathe anymore." I was lucky to get a loving boss. When 'Work Life Balance' was unheard of, my thoughtful Boss taught me that.

Finally, the promotion list was out and as expected, I was promoted to Branch Manager, but the icing on the cake was my posting to Nagpur, my hometown. We all were happy and eager to go to Nagpur and stay in our own house with our mother. Almost every day we had a farewell dinner from someone or the other. Kolhapur has a unique style of preparing mutton and more than that, serving it to guests with affection. I haven't eaten such delicious non-vegetarian food in my life. A good number of friends, office colleagues, Agents had gathered at the railway station to see us off. The two years spent in Kolhapur, in the marketing wing made my foundation in marketing solid which helped my career in the future. We always become nostalgic when we remember Kolhapur.

Lessons Learnt...

- Revise what you have learnt in the day, before going to bed, even if it's a quick read. It will give you confidence when there's a surprise test or a presentation to be made.
- Savings is not what remains at the end of the month but it is what you set aside at the beginning of the month and manage your expenses with the balance left.
- Business will happen but taking care of family is also equally important.
- Avoid being superstitious.
- Strike a chord with customers.

IV

Nagpur – Pune – Solapur

We were happy to get a posting in Nagpur for multiple reasons. Our ancestral house was in Nagpur where my mother was staying alone since the tenants who were staying there had vacated recently. We had absolutely no intention of staying in the LIC officers' quarters although the same were available. Secondly, Nilambari's parents and two brothers with their children were staying at a walking distance from our house. We were back home after almost five years. When I left Nagpur five years ago, I was a clerk while today I was a Branch Manager with a car and a telephone. It was a proud moment and a prestigious posting for me. We could have stayed in Nagpur till my next promotion which was due after five years but due to a foolish act on my part, I was transferred out after just two years. Anyways, everything happens for the good.

As I had completed five years of service in LIC, I was eligible to apply for a housing loan. Since we had a house in Nagpur, we decided to buy a flat in another city. We told our relatives in Pune to be on the lookout for a flat in Pune's Kothrud area. I was informed that M/s A V Bhat, a reputed builder from Pune had announced a housing scheme of over a hundred flats near the Cummins' factory in Dahanukar Colony, Pune. I immediately rushed to Pune, paid a token amount and booked a 430 sq. ft. flat in Shubh Nagari society for ₹2.40 lakh. My loan eligibility was

₹1.60 lakh and I had to pay the balance amount in stages as the flat was under construction and was likely to be ready for occupation in eighteen to twenty months. Arranging about a lakh of rupees was a difficult proposition then, but my father-in-law, Mr B C Sane and my mother came to the rescue. Also, Nilambari pledged all her gold to a bank and raised ₹20,000. Somehow, without defaulting on any instalment, we managed to pay the agreement price in the given time frame and we received the letter from the builder in May 1990 asking us to take possession of the flat. It was a coincidence that my transfer order to Pune as Branch Manager, 955 Br. was also received on the same day. We were, no doubt, happy that we would be able to stay in the newly constructed flat in Pune, but were not delighted as we had to leave Nagpur in just two years. But more on that later.

After we had settled in Nagpur, Himanshu's admission was finalised in Bishop Cotton School in the Class I and Kaustubh got admission in Jr.KG in Mount Carmel School where Tai's daughter, Mukta was studying in the Class V. Children started going to school by rickshaw. Nilambari was posted to a Branch which was just two to three kilometres away. She started going to her office on a Luna moped and I used to drive my car to the Branch at Sadar which was about five to six kilometres away.

Sadar Branch was quite notorious for the bad behaviour of some employees. They treated the Branch Manager as if he was their personal servant and they would harass, insult and demean the officers to the extent that the Branch Manager would request a transfer out of the Branch. I was a young and local Branch Manager. There was no reason for me to be afraid of them or to succumb to their pressure.

One day, a senior Development Officer (DO) Mr P C Agrawal entered my cabin virtually pouncing on me and shouting. He was a firebrand leader of the Development Officers and I could sense that he wanted to show his supremacy, while he was shouting. "Why is this proposal not completed? It should have been completed two days ago. You have no control over your staff..." In my mind I was planning my strategy to teach him a lesson. I said, "Mr Agrawal, don't forget that you are speaking to your senior. Lower your voice." He said, "Such is my normal voice. You will have to listen to what I say." I called a sub staff and asked him to move his chair to the door which was about ten feet from my chair. I said, "Mr Agrawal, if you cannot speak in a lower tone, go sit in that chair which is at the door and say what you want to say in your normal voice. I don't want to become deaf due to hearing your high pitch voice. Go, sit there and speak." He was burning with anger but had no alternative. He never thought that I would literally show him the door. His tone of voice came down. He said, "Sir, you got upset for no reason. We want to see that the work is done." I said, "Yes, that is my responsibility and if you present yourself in a decent and respectful way, your job will be done else don't enter my cabin henceforth." By that time a few DOs and staff members had entered my cabin. He wanted to show them that he was a tiger but they found him turned into a sheep. They too never liked his arrogance but were helpless. Inwardly, they felt happy that a bold and courageous Branch Manager had come to choke the voice of the troublemaker. Mr Agarwal became quite friendly with me thereafter. Our Branch achieved its budget. The next year was easier for me, since I was able to get a good grip over the working of the Branch. Although the Branch performance was extremely good in the next year as well, out of the blue, my transfer order was issued by the Zonal Office.

We hoped to continue in Nagpur for four to five years till the next promotion. But that was not to happen. I was transferred in just two years. How and why? I have to curse myself for the foolishness I did on Republic Day of 1990.

As per the prevailing practice, after the Flag hoisting at the hands of Sr. Divisional Manager (SDM) on the terrace of National Insurance Building which housed the Nagpur Divisional office, SDM used to address the gathering for five to ten minutes followed by tea and snacks. Mr Samuel Alexander was SDM.

He had no exposure to marketing in the past but was an upright and honest officer. After the flag hoisting, we were eager to listen to the motivational speech from our SDM. About two hundred people had gathered since many staff members had brought their spouses and children for the function. The SDM started his speech with opening remarks, "Dear LIC colleagues, who says LIC is not corrupt?" Everyone present there was dumbfounded. We could not understand what he meant. To explain his point he added, "You are all supposed to work for about six hours every day but I find that you reach office late, leave early, spend more time on lunch, frequently take breaks for tea and *paan* (tobacco). Thus, you work only for four and a half hours daily and, hence, you are corrupt to that extent."

We were taken aback and we decided to submit a memorandum explaining to him that what he said in his speech, in front of staff's family members and children, was inappropriate. They could have easily misunderstood him and might have thought that their 'corrupt' father is working for a 'corrupt' organisation.

We drafted a letter on the letterhead of the Class 1 Officers' Association condemning his speech and the next day we went to hand it over to him. The delegation was led by Peter Pinto, Prabodh Yelne (13th Batch Officer) and me. We met him. He read the letter, his face turned red and he simply threw the letter in the dustbin saying, "You are not supposed to teach me what I should speak and what not. I have observed that indiscipline is rampant here." To this I said, "Sir, you are the Disciplinary Authority and it is your responsibility to discipline the staff. Calling all employees corrupt was improper on the occasion of Republic Day."

"Don't advise me, Mr Sathe. You may leave now."

On coming back home, when I narrated it to Nilambari, she said, "You will suffer for this act of foolishness. Be ready."

In April 1990 the transfer orders were issued. Mr Pinto was sent to Nashik; Mr Yelne, just a year after his posting, was sent to Aurangabad while I was transferred to 955 Br. Pune. He thus ensured that three of us go to three different places.

In 1992, I was due for promotion. I was not expecting my name in the list due to the fiasco that I created two years back while in Nagpur. To my surprise I got the promotion on time. It was clear that although Mr Samuel Alexander ensured that I was shunted out of Nagpur, at the same time, he ensured my promotion by writing an excellent Confidential Report (CR) for me despite my foolishness. I was lucky to have such a large hearted boss who did not let one incident affect my career.

As I mentioned earlier, it was a great coincidence that my transfer orders to Pune and the letter from the builder that our flat in Pune was ready for possession reached me on the same day. We decided to shift quickly to Pune. I joined 955 Br. and Nilambari got a posting in Pune DO. It took over a month to get her transfer order issued, till then she was on leave. Although in general, the image of Puneites is that they don't help others, they consider others as lesser mortals, they are sceptical and sarcastic when they speak but for us the experience was totally different. Mr Rajabhau Chitley, an employee of Pune DO was helpful in getting admission for my children in Class I and Class III in Karnatak High school. Our neighbours, Mr and Mrs Phadke assured us that they would ensure that children would be well taken care of before their school rickshaw came and also till the time one of us would return from office. Since Shubh Nagari was a colony with over a hundred flats, the children made new friends. They quickly adjusted to school as well. We had a house warming ceremony for which my mother, sister and many relatives and acquaintances had assembled. We had a good number of relatives and friends in Pune. Visiting them, or exploring the surrounding places of interest on Sundays and holidays became quite a routine for us.

I had excellent office colleagues. The Branch staff was dominated by ladies. Almost ninety per cent of the staff was female and most of them were hard-working and the Branch was administratively, one of the best Branches of Pune DO. Many staff members and officers used to come to the Branch on Sundays and holidays to clear their pending work.

On 14 April 1992 it was a holiday on account of Ambedkar *Jayanti*, but due to year end work that needed to be completed, almost thirty per cent of the staff and two of the officers, Mr Wamanrao Kangne and Mr Vijayanand Kamble had come to office along with me. At about 2:00 pm, we decided to go out for lunch. When we were coming down in the lift, we observed that a poster pasted in the lift about Babasaheb Ambedkar was badly defaced by some antisocial element. We deemed it improper to keep it on display there and hence when we reached the ground floor, we decided to remove it. I tore it off and put it in the dustbin near the lift. Mr Kangne returned to the office with me after our lunch while Mr Kamble left as he had some other assignment. We worked in the office till 6:30 or 7:00 pm and went home.

The next morning, I got a call from Mr Baliga SDM Pune. He said, "Nilesh, did you tear off the poster of Babasaheb from the lift yesterday?" I said, "Yes, I did" and told him the reason for the same. He said, "I have received a complaint and I am sending Mr Agashe, ADM to investigate the matter and submit his report. He will reach there soon." I called both the officers who were with me in the lift when the poster was removed. They were shocked and never thought that it would take such a serious turn. What we did was for the good but had no evidence to prove it. We guessed that the watchman on the ground floor must have played the mischief. Mr Kamble, who himself belonged to the scheduled caste, got so furious that he said, "Let Mr Agashe come. I will tell him whatever I have to say. You don't utter a single word." When Mr Agashe came, Mr Kamble said, "Sir, it was not Mr Sathe but I myself tore off the poster as it was defaced and keeping it there might have given rise to social upheaval and unrest. Mr Kangne and Mr Sathe were present when I did it. My intention was noble but still if you want to take any action, take it against me and not against Mr Sathe." Report was accordingly submitted and the matter was closed. Such were my colleagues and I owe them a lot.

On account of my good performance at the Branch, I was promoted and transferred to 944 Br. Solapur as Sr. Branch Manager. The Branch was known as a notorious Branch which

I noticed on the day of my joining itself. There was a notice board for the staff unions. A notice was displayed there which must have been put up for almost a week as my predecessor had left a week before I joined. The notice read: "Our Sr.BM, Mr..... is no more. Please assemble today at the Branch ground at 5:30 pm to pay condolences."

I wanted to find the reason for transferring me to such a notorious Branch. I went to Mumbai to meet Mr V C Desai who was Regional Manager (P&IR) Western Zonal Office. He was Marketing Manager at Satara DO when I was at Sangli Br. as AAO. We knew each other, rather he was my role model. He was a no-nonsense person and was an expert on HR matters. When I met him, he said, "Nilesh, I knew that you would come to meet me to find why I posted you to 944 Br. Solapur." He called some officer and asked him to get Mr Baliga's (SDM Pune) recommendations file on posting. He opened a page from the file and asked me to read it. Mr Baliga had written about me as follows, "In our division we have a Branch 944 Solapur which is the most notorious Branch. Over a hundred Audit Query Slips (AQS) are pending. In the past six years audit reports are not yet closed, unions are overactive, staff is arrogant and indisciplined. I have no officer before me other than Nilesh Sathe who has the capability to set things right. He is due for promotion and is likely to be promoted. If promoted or otherwise, I recommend the posting of Mr Sathe as Branch Manager in charge of 944 Br." When I finished reading it, Mr Desai said, "Even I did not get such a certificate in my life. You are capable, confident and tactful. You are the best choice. Mr Baliga's assessment is proper." I felt elated due to the kind words of Mr Baliga and Mr Desai.

Since it was a transfer within the Division, Nilambari's transfer was effected immediately. Both of us left Pune on the same day with all our belongings since residential quarters were already vacant at Solapur. By this time we were used to transfers and just in a couple of days, we finished routine work of surrendering the gas connection, removing the names of our children from their school, arranging movers and packers etc. We reached Solapur by car following the truck carrying our luggage. Three of my office colleagues, development officers, Milind Mane, Vijay Kadam and Mohan Awale came by a separate car to Solapur to help us arrange our belongings in the quarters. The quarters were on the second floor with five spacious rooms and were just behind the Branch where I was posted. Our children got admission in Saint Joseph's High School which was very close to our residence.

Some of the employees of the Branch were actually mischievous. When I asked someone as to why the Auditors have issued so many Audit Query Slips (AQS) in the Sales Department, what I heard was unimaginable. He said, "The Auditor was sitting on a chair. Behind him was a rack and on the top shelf there was a pile of files. He asked Mr Kulkarni to give him one of those files. Mr Kulkarni simply said, 'It's just behind you, why don't you stand on your chair and take it yourself'. The Auditor still insisted that the file be given to him. Very reluctantly Kulkarni got up from his seat and pulled the file which was at the bottom of the pile in such a way that all the thick files, may be weighing seven to eight kilograms fell on the Auditor's head. "Sir, do you still think that the AQS issued for the Sales department were a lot?" Both of us had a hearty laugh.

On the day when I joined the Branch, I went from table to table, shook hands with the employees and got to know their names and the department to which they were attached. I then went to the cash counter at the entrance of the Branch. The Union's notice board was also there. It was a glass cabinet with a lock. I found the notorious 'condolence' notice displayed there. I called the one who had signed it and said, "Now since the earlier Branch Manager has left and a week has passed thereafter, remove the notice." I knew that it was intentionally kept there to make me aware of the way unions treated the officers. I was undeterred. I asked him the reason for such undemocratic, insulting language used for my predecessor. He told me how the earlier BM thought that if disciplinary action was taken against the employees, peace would prevail. But that was not the case. Things worsened during his two year regime. Hence they condemned him.

On the first day itself I saw that all the staff members including the cashiers left at 12:30 pm to have a cup of tea. It took me some time to realise that the Branch was deserted. Lunch time was from 2:00 pm to 2:30 pm. When there was a deafening silence, I came out of my cabin to find a few customers at the cash counter waiting for the cashiers to come back from their tea sojourn. Such a scene was never seen in the past in any of the Branches I worked in and was unheard of. During office time, without permission, all staff members leaving their seats together for half an hour made me alert and aware of the faith imposed on me by Mr Baliga, SDM. It was time for me to act fast. If I tolerate it on day one, I would be taken for granted. I decided to stand at the entrance of the Branch till all of them walked in. At about 1:00 pm they began entering. Most of them had a guilty feeling. I made them stand outside the entrance and after all had assembled, I said, "I agree that one needs a break after working for two hours in the morning. But making policyholders wait for payment of premium is criminal. We get our salary because they pay premiums. I do not want the entire Branch to be deserted for half an hour. Each department should have at least one person in his seat including the cashier. Out of two cashiers, you decide amongst yourself as to who will go out for tea first and the other will leave his seat only when the first cashier returns to his seat. I want you to follow this practice." I returned to my cabin without giving them a chance to argue or counter me.

My cabin had a cash safe. After the day's transactions were tallied, the cashiers along with their officer would come to my cabin, open the safe with two keys, place the cash in the safe, close it and leave. It was a routine practice. That day I stopped the cashiers and made them sit before me. I said, "Don't you think that it's inhumane to make customers wait during office hours? In case you go to some Government office and find that the concerned staff is missing for a long time, will you not curse them? Is there any problem if one of you leaves only when the other cashier has returned from his tea break?"

"Sir, we have no problem. But this practice is followed in our Branch for many years and our union leader wants to ensure that the practice continues. You tell the union leader. If he agrees, we have no objection in following your instructions." Without allowing them to go, I called the union leader on the intercom and asked him to come to my cabin immediately. When he came, I said, "From tomorrow these two cashiers have agreed to go for tea one at a time. I called you only to reaffirm what I said in the afternoon at the entrance. From tomorrow, all of you will not go at the same time. You may form two groups and the second group will leave only when the first group returns."

"This tradition has been going on here for the last twenty years. You have come today. Just by your orders, we will not change the tradition. You don't interfere, please."

"Comrade leader, I have been posted here with a purpose. I have told you that the cash counter will not close for half an hour. The two cashiers will not leave at the same time. Hope this is understood. You may leave now."

I learnt that the Comrade leader called for a meeting after office hours and said, "The new BM is trying to put an end to our tradition of going together for tea. We should stand united and ensure that his divisive politics fails." The same was reported to me by a comrade of another rival group. My Plan B was ready. The next day, five minutes before their usual time of 12:30 pm. I came out of my cabin and stood at the cash counter. I asked them, "Who is going first?" I told the customers standing in the queue that this cashier will leave after five minutes so they should stand in the queue in front of the other cashier. I asked the officer to make a notice that read 'This counter will close at 12:30 pm'. I asked him to display it at the counter of the first cashier. For the second cash counter, I asked him to display the board that read 'This counter will close at 1:00 pm'. I stood there to find that the first cashier alone leaves at 12:30 pm. I repeated it for the next two to three days and thereafter it became a practice. Office staff started leaving in two groups. As I started enforcing discipline, newer issues cropped up.

It is not that the Branch had no sincere and hardworking staff but the reputation of the Branch was so bad that no one from the Branch had received a promotion during the last four to five years. I made special effort to ensure that at least one deserving candidate gets a promotion from the Branch which motivated the good workers to do better.

I helped some employees get housing loan, vehicle loan, loan against their Provident Fund etc. by using my good relations with the Pune Divisional Office. These employees respected me and would never say 'No' to me.

But still some employees continued to be trouble makers. One day, the officer in charge of Finance and Accounts came to me and said, "Sir, tomorrow one cashier wants to be on leave. As per the panel of cashiers, it was Mr Swamy's turn but when I called him to take charge, he refused. The next person on the panel is also refusing because he feels it's unfair to him." I said, "You ask Mr Swamy to see me." Mr Swamy came. It was about half an hour before closing time. I asked him, "Mr Swamy, do you know that as per the cashiers' panel it is your turn to be the 'acting cashier' tomorrow? I heard that you refused to take charge. Is it true?" He said, "Yes, I don't want to work as a cashier tomorrow. Do whatever you want to do."

"Is your decision final?"

"Yes."

In front of him, I called the stenographer and dictated to her a letter addressed to Mr Swamy which was as follows, "Although as per the panel of cashiers, it was your turn to act as officiating cashier on (date), you refused to take cash keys. This is gross misconduct. I am hereby suspending you from the services of the Corporation with immediate effect." In ten minutes the stenographer brought the typed letter. In front of the concerned officer, I issued the suspension order to Mr Swamy, took his acknowledgement and only then allowed him to leave my cabin. I told the officer to keep the keys with him without signing on the register called Daily Cash Balance Book (DCB). When I was about to leave office at about

6:00 pm, the union leader with two or three of his side-kicks came to my cabin. He said, "Sir, do you know that you are just a Sr. BM while the power to suspend an employee vests only with Mr Baliga, the Sr. DM. Your action is high-handed and it is in your interest that you should take back Mr Swamy's order of suspension."

I said, "Look, I know what my rights, duties and obligations are. You don't have to teach me. I am reporting to Sr. DM and not to you. I have issued the order of suspension and I will not take it back. Do what you want to do. You may go now." When they left, I called the editor of Tarun Bharat, Mr Vivek Ghalsasi whom I knew personally. The newspaper had wide circulation in Solapur. I took his time and met him. I said, "Vivek, I need your help." I told him about the undisciplined behaviour of the employees and requested him to give the news of Mr Swamy's suspension on the front page. Since I had the signed suspension order as evidence, he had no problem.

On reaching home, at about 9:00 pm, I got a call from Mr Baliga, SDM Pune who said, "Nilesh, the Staff Union has complained to me that you suspended one employee at Solapur today. Don't you know that the authority to suspend a Class 3 employee vests with me and not with you?" I told him why I did so and requested him to give me twenty-four hours within which I would either withdraw the order or make Swamy accept his cashier duties. I had full support of Mr Baliga. I could know from his tone that he was smiling, he advised me to go ahead. You need to have full support of your boss if you want to decide on matters sometimes beyond your authority. I was fortunate to have good bosses.

The next day, an hour before office timing, Mr Swamy came to my residence with folded hands and almost in tears saying, "Sir, I made a mistake. I should not have refused to work as the officiating cashier. Please revoke my suspension. After reading the news in the newspaper, all my relatives are questioning me. They are thinking that I have committed a fraud. I have no face to show in our community. I am ready to work as a cashier." I asked him to reach the Branch fifteen minutes before the start of cash hours.

I also reached office at that time. The officer in charge of cash had also come. I asked Mr Swamy to sign the DCB of the previous day and take the keys of the cash and be seated at the cashier's counter. I took the copy of the letter of suspension from him and tore it off along with his acknowledgement of the order. When the Comrade leader came, he saw Mr Swamy at the cash counter. He asked him about why he was working as cashier to which Mr Swamy told him that he would never refuse any of my orders thereafter. The union leader had come prepared to wage war against me but found that his disciple had surrendered even before the war had started.

The Branch was improving, business was picking up. I was enjoying my job. On the family front, as well, children were doing well at school. They learnt swimming, badminton, table tennis. In May 1994 we arranged their thread ceremony at Solapur. Most of our relatives came for the function. I had arranged a trip to Bijapur to show them the historical cannon and Gol Gumbaz.

My mother, in the meanwhile, retired from Hadas High School and came to stay with us permanently. These were the formative years of the children and their grandmother's presence in the house was of great help to us.

My marketing stint of eight years was coming to an end. I was expecting a transfer but we never expected that I would be transferred out of Maharashtra. We were really upset when we saw my posting to Kolkata (formerly Calcutta) in the transfer order. But there was no option. We were told that in Kolkata schools reopen in April. It was June when I got the orders. Hence we decided to move to Kolkata immediately since quarters in Kolkata were reported to be available. We sent the luggage to Nagpur first and another truck carried it to Kolkata. We also went to Nagpur first, and from there, after seeing that the Kolkata bound truck had left Nagpur, we boarded the Bombay-Howrah Express to start a new journey to 'Aamar Shonar Bangla'.

Before we left, the staff members and Agents erected a pandal on the Branch ground to arrange a grand farewell for me and surprisingly all union leaders were sharing the dais; they all spoke highly of me. One staff member remarked, “Mr Sathe brought the Branch on track and, in the process, he also earned goodwill. He did take disciplinary actions but ensured that the employees’ interests are always protected.” When I was listening to all the praise that was being heaped on me, I was reminded of my first day in the Branch when I had seen a circular displayed on notice board by one of the unions saying, “Our Sr. BM, Mr..... is no more. Please assemble on Branch ground at 5:30 pm to pay condolences.”

My two years term at Solapur is the most memorable one. I had taken the challenge to improve the Branch administration and I am happy I successfully steered the Branch towards it.

Lessons Learnt...

- If you want to decide on matters which are beyond your authority, it’s important to have full support of your Boss.
- It is important to know your rights but it’s equally important to know your duties and responsibilities.
- Be bold to do things which are right.
- Discipline is essential for any organisation to flourish.
- Being capable, confident and tactful are important qualities of a Manager, groom them.
- Be polite but be firm as well. It’s not either or.
- When someone admits his mistake and asks for another chance to improve, give him one more chance, if possible.

V

Aamar Shonar Kolkata

On reaching Kolkata, initially we stayed in a hotel till we received the keys of the quarters allotted to us. Although I ate non-vegetarian food, since Aai was with us, we used to order only vegetarian food. But to our surprise, whenever it was being served, it was accompanied by a typical smell of fish. It was quite irritating for Aai. She hardly used to eat any food. Once she jokingly said, "In Maharashtra, just as we top-up our dishes with grated coconut and coriander leaves, it seems that Bengalis add fish essence to top-up their vegetarian dishes."

After two days, on completing the formalities of allotment of quarters, I was handed over keys of a flat which was at a walking distance from my office. I was quite happy that though not so close, as it was in Solapur, the office was just at a distance of two hundred metres. I went to the flat with the keys that were handed over to me. When I turned the handle and opened the door it opened with a creaking sound as heard in horror movies. It was no less than a 'Ghost House'. It looked as if it was unoccupied for a long period. Cobwebs were hanging, lizards were merrily moving on the walls. It was full of dust. The ceiling was at a height of thirty feet. It was really scary.

I went back to the office and requested the Estate Department to allot me a different flat. The officer not only refused to do so but said, "Sir, if you do not take possession of this flat, it may take at least two to three months for the next flat to be vacant. Please listen to my advice, spend some money, get the flat cleaned and start staying there."

I went to the hotel, discussed the matter with Nilambari and we decided to occupy it as the children's admission into good schools was our top priority and it was becoming increasingly impossible for Aai to get proper vegetarian food which did not have the smell of fish. It was quite costly as well to continue to stay in a hotel.

We bought a bucket, cleaning material, brooms etc., and after literally putting in hard labour for about four hours made the house habitable and we moved in on the same day to start our life in Kolkata. We had a stove and a few utensils with us. Our neighbours helped us with a few more utensils and Nilambari started a make-shift kitchen.

The truck carrying our household goods should have reached by then but there was a delay. As there were no mobile phones in those days, I personally went to the transporter's office in Howrah. My throat dried up and legs started trembling when I heard that the truck had toppled near Raipur, about three hundred kilometres from Nagpur. As the driver didn't have much cash with him, he was unable to arrange a JCB to get the truck back on its wheels. I was told that even after the truck was put back on its wheels, it might take four to five days to reach Kolkata. My heart sank. I came home and went to the public telephone booth to call my cousin Sagar Ashirgade who was to bring my car by road from Nagpur. He was to leave Nagpur for Kolkata the following week. But I asked him to carry some extra cash and leave immediately. I gave him the truck number and the location where the truck was reported to have toppled. He took his friend with him and left soon thereafter. He met the driver, arranged to get the truck back on its wheels, gave him some money and reached Kolkata after two days.

We were advised to get our children's admission done in an ICSE/ CBSE affiliated school. In Maharashtra, those days, most of the schools were affiliated to Maharashtra State Board. We were not aware of ICSE affiliated schools. I took leave for ten days and we were visiting schools in the vicinity but had no success in getting admission as every school Principal said, "Sorry, you are too late. Three months are over. The first unit test is round the corner." One school offered to give them admission in the same class which they had passed at Solapur.

We went to Calcutta Boys School. After a long wait, we were able to get an audience with the Principal. The Principal was a Jesuit, wearing a white robe. He was quite stout, resembling Oliver Hardy from 'Laurel and Hardy'. Sitting in the chair adjacent to him was a jet black bulldog. He was continuously patting the dog. It was difficult to decide, who was more fierce looking, the Dog or the Principal? I submitted my application to him and said, "We got late because our transfers are effected only in May, schools in Maharashtra reopen in June, we were not aware of the fact that the schools in Kolkata reopened in April. The children's mark lists would reflect that they are good at studies. We desperately want them to be admitted to your esteemed school without further loss of time..." I was trying to observe if the Father was moved by my persuasion. After I finished, he said, "Admission is not possible, you may leave now." I continued requesting him further to interview the children or subject them to an entrance exams etc. But still he looked unmoved. When I was about to plead further, Nilambari whispered in my ears in Marathi, "Now if you say one more word, the dog will be signalled to pounce on you." I had a smile on my face and we left his cabin hurriedly glancing back to see whether the dog was following us, making up our minds not to step into that school again! We even tried a free school but based on our appearance and hearing us speak good English, we were turned down. We realized that the free schools were meant for the poor. Our nightmare was partly over when Himanshu got admission in Saint Joseph's School (affiliated to ICSE) but the Father repeatedly said, "No! No! No!" for Kaustubh. Half the job was done. Himanshu started going to school. After three or four days, when we came home from office, we found Kaustubh sobbing uncontrollably. When asked, he said,

"*Dada* (elder brother) has started going to school. When will my school start? Are you planning to keep me at home?" I consoled him and promised that by next week, he would also start going to school, although there was no indication from any school about admitting him. But someone in the office told me to approach a nearby school run by YWCA which had permission only up to Class VII and was affiliated to the CBSE Board. Students from this school used to move to other schools which had further schooling, so there was a possibility of getting admission. I immediately went there. They were more than happy to give Kaustubh admission as later we found that Kaustubh's Class III had only fifteen students. Since getting admission was more important than weighing the other aspects, we paid the fees, bought books, a uniform, and a school bag for him and from the next day, we saw his smiling face ready to go to school. The marathon effort of school admission thus had a happy ending.

Both the children had to catch-up with the lessons they had missed. In just a week or ten days from joining their respective schools, they had a unit test in which both of them secured good marks. They liked their schools but the syllabus was quite tough as compared to State Board. My mother started teaching them languages, I helped with Maths while Nilambari taught them Science. In the annual exam, Kaustubh stood first while Himanshu was in the top ten. We shifted Kaustubh to a better school, Park English School the next year where he had to compete with fifty students in his class.

Nilambari, in the meanwhile joined the Provident Fund Department in the Zonal Office. I was Assistant Secretary (HRD) in the same office. We started going to the office together. My job here was a bit different. I had, along with two others in the department, to conduct HRD sessions for the officers of the entire zone which involved Bihar, Odisha, West Bengal and the seven north eastern states. I used to talk about how to interact with the customers, how not to lose temper even if a customer shouts, how counselling helps in the office as well as at home, problem solving techniques etc. Initially I had to read a lot and search for case studies to prepare notes and PPTs, but soon my module was ready and I found that the officers used to enjoy my sessions. There used to be a lot of questions asked on the Malhotra Committee report which was submitted to the Government of India in 1994. The Committee had recommended the opening up of the insurance sector to private and foreign players.

In one of my training sessions in Guwahati Division, I made a controversial remark, "We ourselves are responsible for this. We only forced the Government to set up such a committee. We acted in the most irresponsible manner. When the Government wanted computerization, we opposed it. The Unions in Kolkata opposed the unloading of the trucks carrying mainframe computers which then finally had to be shifted to Mumbai. The EDP Department in Mumbai has over 700 officers. We lost job opportunities for the youngsters from the Eastern part of India to that extent. We opposed computerization but quietly accepted an extra increment. Our unions misled us and they are also equally responsible for the opening of the insurance sector in India..."

Mr Lalit Kumar Dash was the Senior Divisional Manager of Guwahati. He had come to join us for dinner. At the dinner table he asked me about the reasons I gave for the opening up of the insurance sector in India. I told him what I had said in the class. He smiled and said, "The union's approach has still not changed. I received a complaint from their leaders and they have asked me to convey to you their displeasure."

"Sir, do you want me to stop saying so?"

He laughed, "Nilesh, they wanted me to convey their displeasure which I have conveyed. Did I ask you to stop saying what you said? Actually, I wanted someone to tell them this. It's good that you are taking the bull by its horns. Well done! Keep it up."

It was a very satisfying tour of ten days to Guwahati. I was thirty-nine then but you may be surprised that I had never travelled by air before. LIC was allowing air travel on tour only to officers of DM rank and above. I was an ADM rank officer but for travelling to places in the North East, all the officers irrespective of their rank were allowed to travel by air. Thus, I had my first air travel experience from Kolkata to Guwahati. The Brahmaputra river from the window of the plane looked like an ocean.

One of my jobs was to visit Branches and conduct customer satisfaction surveys. A bilingual questionnaire in Bengali and English was prepared by Professor Ishwar Dayal who was a Management Consultant for LIC. One day I reached Howrah Branch at 9:45 am as the cash counter of the Branch was to open at 10:00 am. A few customers were waiting in the seating lounge, for the cashier to arrive. They had come to pay the premium on their policies. I saw a dhoti clad Bengali Babu chewing paan and smoking a cigarette. By the time he had smoked the cigarette and spit the paan juice at the gate of the Branch, it was 10:10 am but the cashier had not arrived. I gave him my card and asked him if he would like to answer a few questions in the customer satisfaction Survey. On getting his nod, I asked him the questions and noted his answers. After all the questions were answered, I read over the replies that I had noted and took his signature. It was 10:30 am and finally the cash counter had opened. I asked him, "Dada, don't you get aggrieved and agitated that you had to waste 30 minutes due to the cashier not coming on time?" What he answered, not only amused me but it gave a new dimension to the survey report. He said, "Sir, this is the only office where nothing over and above the amount mentioned in the 'Notice' (premium notice), is asked for."

He further said, "What else is required? Moreover, if you talk of delay, take my case. My office opens at 10:00 am. I am leaving from here at 10.45 am and will reach my seat by 11.15 am. I will also reach my office late. What is so special about it?"

It opened a different vista of looking at the survey, I inferred that the level of customer satisfaction varies from place to place. It depends on the efficiency of the employees but more than that, it depends on the expectations of the customers. The report was discussed in the next meeting in Mumbai; my observation was much appreciated.

I also observed that the demands of union were never ending when I had a chance to conduct HRD sessions at Jamshedpur. I was privy to the unfortunate incident that happened in the Divisional Office, Jamshedpur where my friend, Mr S K Roy, Manager (P&IR) along with me were *Gheraoed* (surrounded from all sides) by employees for half an hour.

It so happened that one day after my last lecture, I was free at 4:30 pm when Mr Roy said, "Nilesh, I have some work left in the office, as it is, you are free now, why don't you accompany me?" We went on his scooter, to the DO building which was three to four kilometres from the venue where the session was being held. As we were climbing the steps to the first floor, suddenly many employees gathered around and *gheraoed* us making it impossible for us to either go down or climb up the stairs. They started shouting slogans. The drama continued for over half an hour. Afterwards, the Union Leader came close to Mr Roy and asked him, "How have you effected transfer of a certain employee without taking our consent? You listen to the leaders of the other Unions and ignore us? That won't be tolerated. You must take back the transfer order." Although he addressed Mr Roy in Bengali, by then I had learnt enough Bengali to understand what he said. Mr Roy was unperturbed. He kept repeating, "Give your demands in writing. I will put them up before the Sr DM." They were not relenting. Finally, after forty minutes or so of the *gherao*, Mr Roy said, "You all have wasted more than half an hour during office time which may warrant action against all of you." To this the Union Leader said, "Don't think that some employee affiliated with the other Union will stand as witness against us. All Unions have this understanding with each other. No case can stand without a proper witness."

The Union Leader had brought the representation but didn't give it in the beginning. He wanted to show his strength. He gave it to Mr Roy and rudely said, "We want you to act fast on our representation else you will have to face serious consequences."

He asked the employees to allow us to leave. We went to Mr Roy's cabin. He said, "Nilesh, what he said is correct. These Unions will fight with each other but will never allow management to initiate action against a Union Leader. Let us first go to Mr P K Mishra, Sr DM, and report the matter to him." Mr Mishra, heard patiently what Mr Roy reported. He was an upright and bold officer. He said, "As you suggest, I have no hesitation in taking action against the employees who did this. But in the absence of an eye witness, the case won't stand."

"Sir, if you allow me, I am ready to be the witness. There cannot be a more independent witness than me as I am not an officer of your Division," I said.

Mr Mishra's face brightened. He said, "Mr Roy, if that is the case, you propose the action to be taken against those employees."

We left his cabin. Mr Roy prepared a report of the incident. I witnessed it. He prepared a note suggesting suspension of the Union leader along with a few others, took it to Mr Mishra and for the first time in the history of the Jamshedpur Division, the Sr DM issued orders suspending the Union Leader and a few employees. My friendship with Mr S K Roy strengthened after that incident. Mr Roy later went on to become the Chairman of LIC.

I had almost completed my three year tenure in Kolkata. I was due for promotion as Divisional Manager (DM). During our stay in Kolkata, we picked up Bengali reasonably well. Kaustubh used to write Bengali flawlessly as he studied the language in school for three years. One day he returned from school extremely delighted because his Bengali language teacher showed his Bengali handwriting to the boys in the class and patted him for having better handwriting than most of the Bengali students.

I was expecting an elevation in my career but did not want to continue in the Eastern Zone. In school Himanshu had reached Class X and Kaustubh Class VIII. We thought that if they passed Class X and Class XII from Maharashtra, they will be considered as Domiciles of Maharashtra state and it would benefit them to get college admissions for higher studies. I had come to Mumbai in March 1997 to attend a wedding when I met Mr S C Jain, Chief (Personnel) who assured me of my transfer to Maharashtra since I was completing my three year tenure out of my parent zone. We were eagerly waiting to go back.

One day, our maid, while sweeping our drawing room, found a baby owl sitting below the bed. She was so delighted to find it in the house that she went running to the kitchen to give Nilambari the news. It was Sunday so the children were at home. All of us assembled in the drawing room. She lovingly picked up the owl and said, "Madam, the owl is the vehicle of Goddess Lakshmi. It's a good omen, something good is soon going to happen to you. It's very auspicious."

Nilambari was worried how to drive it out. We had a notion that an Owl cannot see in day light. The maid, who was Bengali, was keen to take it home to which quickly and happily Nilambari agreed.

A few days later, we received the good news of my promotion along with my posting to Mumbai. Aai was very happy since she had fond memories of her four to five years stay in Mumbai. Himanshu was upset because he had to leave his friends after being together for three years. I was posted in Central Office as Deputy Secretary in the Pension & Group Schemes (P&GS) Dept. I had never worked in this Dept in the past, nor in the Central Office. So, I was delighted to get a chance to learn something new and also to work closely with the top officials of LIC.

My father's uncle, Upendra alias Anna Sathe was the President of Parle Tilak Vidyalaya Association in Mumbai which ran a renowned school in Vile Parle named Parle Tilak Vidyalaya which was affiliated to the Maharashtra State Board. I was likely to get quarters in Santacruz and as such getting admission in a nearby school would save the children's commuting time. I had a telephonic conversation with Anna Sathe and requested him to help me in securing admissions for both the children in Parle Tilak Vidyalaya which he happily agreed.

I joined the Central Office, stayed in the LIC Guest House at Churchgate, took possession of the two BHK quarters in Jeevan Shanti Colony, Santacruz and went to Kolkata to wind up and bring my family to Mumbai. Our car was loaded in the same truck which carried our household goods. We had developed friendships with many Bengalis and their families, some of whom are still in touch with us. By and large my posting in Kolkata was an enriching experience. We learnt a new language. With heavy hearts, we boarded the flight to Mumbai and the following words were uttered spontaneously by us 'Aamar Shonar Kolkata'.

Lessons Learnt...

- Sometimes things may not go according to your plan. Learn to adapt and overcome challenging situations.
- Children are more resilient than you think. They adapt and thrive in new settings much faster than we think.
- Never be afraid. Take the bull by its horns.
- The level of customer satisfaction varies from place to place. It depends more on the Customers' expectations than the employees' efficiency.

VI

Mumbai – My Love

The flat allotted to us on the second floor in Jeevan Shanti colony, Santacruz, Mumbai was a spacious 2 BHK flat with two balconies which was enough for our family. As against Kolkata where it was a herculean task to get our children admitted to a new school, in Mumbai it was a cake walk. Kaustubh was in Class VIII and he liked Parle Tilak Vidyalaya, his new school. On the other hand, Himanshu, who was in the Class X, disliked the school to the hilt. He had spent his last three years in a missionary school in Kolkata where the school had a huge football ground. It was a boy's school in Kolkata while the new school in Mumbai was co-ed and most of the teachers were women. In Kolkata his friends used to speak with each other mostly in English and sometimes in Bengali or Hindi while here in the new school even the teachers used to explain the concepts in Marathi. It was a bit difficult for him to make friends as the class boys had their own groups already and Himanshu was the 'odd one out'. He would often grumble to his grandmother, "Why did you bring me here? I would have stayed in Kolkata in a hostel. Nobody here speaks in English in my class and I badly miss football as the school doesn't have a big playground." His grandma being a retired school teacher knew child psychology well and did not allow the situation to get out of hand. She kept him busy with studies and other activities.

Nilambari had requested for a transfer from Kolkata to Mumbai but since it was inter-zonal transfer, it took more than four months to get a posting to Mumbai. She had to be on leave till the time her transfer order was issued. It was good in a way because she could pay attention to the children's studies. She also enrolled in the Parents-Teachers Association which used to help the school when the teachers were on long leave. She used to go to Parle Tilak Vidyalaya daily to take classes up to Class VIII as one teacher was on maternity leave. This continued for over two months till Nilambari was transferred to Mumbai.

As Nilambari was at home for the first four months, I could devote more time to my office work. The work allotted to me was absolutely new for two reasons: one, the insurance that I was well versed with till then was insurance that catered to individuals, whereas now I had to deal with insurance that catered to groups. Obviously, the insurance plans were different and hence the marketing techniques were also different. Secondly my posting was in the Central Office which is a policy making office. Earlier I was on the execution side while now my role was of supervision and control.

I had a varied job profile as Deputy Secretary, Pension and Group Schemes (P&GS) Department, Central Office Mumbai. In addition to the Finance and Accounts Section, I had to look after Social Security schemes, unique schemes referred by P&GS Units for approval, preparing notes for Board meetings etc. I had to study the P&GS manual, learn from senior colleagues, but the most important and challenging assignment was preparing Board Notes and their submission to the Board Secretariat within the given time frame. Mr H O Sonig was Executive Director (ED), P&GS who asked me to go through the past few notes and warned me that the notes should be flawless. I was very careful in compiling data, drafting notes etc. After the first few Board Notes went well, I goofed up once. Due to leaves, holidays, late submission of data by the units, I did not get time to check the notes this time and on approval of ED,

I sent twenty-five copies of the same to the Board Secretariat, a week before the date of the Board meeting. The Board secretariat used to compile the board notes received from all the departments and used to send the spiral–bound notes to all the EDs. Mr Sonig also received the notes a day before the Board meeting. He called me at about 5:00 pm and asked me, "Mr Sathe, I had warned you to be careful while drafting the Board Notes but I find that there is a mistake in the business figures mentioned here." He showed me where the goof up had happened. I apologised and asked him what should be done. There was no point in arguing with him that the note was sent to the Board only after his approval. I could not ask him, "Why didn't you point out the mistake to me before approving the note?" In management, there is a basic principle, 'Never argue with your boss; you may win the argument but lose the promotion'. As per his advice, I took twenty-five copies of the corrected notes to the Board secretariat and requested them to substitute the old one with the corrected one and placed it on the desk of the board members. It was 7:00 pm by then. Mr Sonig was waiting for my confirmation. He was happy that the corrections were carried out quickly but did not miss giving me a sermon. "Mr Sathe, if a Branch makes a mistake, the Divisional Office (DO) can correct it, if DO makes a mistake, it can be corrected by Zonal Office (ZO), if ZO makes a mistake, it can be corrected by Central Office (CO), but once the board note is approved by the Board, there is no scope to correct it and it may mean that we have intentionally tried to mislead the Board. Be careful in the future." I nodded my head. I learnt the lesson which I found useful when Board Notes started going to the board with my approval when I became ED and CEO.

One day, the unit in charge of Mumbai approached me with a proposal of group insurance for the members of Pan Card Club Pvt Ltd. The Agent was quite enthused as the proposal, if approved, would have helped him to get over one lakh lives (when his annual budget itself was less than one lakh). It was referred to me since it involved lives beyond the permissible limit within the approval authority of the unit in charge and also to decide the premium rate. I asked him to leave the file with me and come the next day. I went through the papers. I understood that the club was collecting fixed deposits only of ₹5,000 and ₹10,000 from its members with assurance to refund them ₹10,000 and ₹20,000 respectively after thirty-six months. It was proposed that in case the member died, LIC should pay the maturity amount to the nominee for which the club was ready to pay the premium. I understood that it was a Ponzi scheme with multi-level marketing. Before I could write my views on the proposal, Mr Sudhir Morvekar, the promoter and CMD of the club came to meet me. He was a tall handsome man in his mid-forties with an impressive personality. After exchanging pleasantries, he showed me a glossy booklet of the club. It was an impressive one with his full-size picture with a private jet in the background, which gave the first impression that he was the owner of the jet. The inside pages had details of the fixed deposit scheme. Looking at the glossy and well-made booklet, anyone would have been impressed with him and his scheme. I was not. The scheme was to double the investor's money in three years. I asked him, "Mr Morvekar what is the maximum amount of money that a person can invest in your scheme?" He said "Sir, we accept only ₹5,000 or ₹10,000 per person, mostly from rural areas of Konkan and Marathwada. We want to channelize small savings into high yielding investment but we do not want to accept deposits of more than ₹10,000 from anybody." I immediately understood the hidden agenda. A person will not spend money on litigation if he loses ₹5,000 or ₹10,000. I requested him to explain the scheme to me further. I also wanted to know the amount of commission that would be paid to the procurer.

He said, "Twenty-five per cent. Many Talathis, Gram Sevaks, Political Leaders, Policemen have taken an agency in the name of their wives."

I asked, "Now out of ₹100, ₹25 going as commission and ₹10 as administrative expenses, what remains for investment is only ₹65. Now tell me how ₹65 becomes ₹200 at the end of three years?"

I could see the uneasiness on his face but he tried to hide it. Side stepping my question, he said, "Sir, I have come to you for a group insurance scheme for our depositors. I have a social objective. In case a depositor dies before completion of three years of deposits, I want his family to get a full guaranteed maturity amount. Please quote me the premium for the same. I am ready to pay for it. Moreover, now the real estate sector is booming, and the hotel industry is on the rise. I will invest there." I was not convinced. I told him that I would discuss the proposal with my seniors and would inform him of the decision the next day. He left but before going he showed me a list of directors on the board of Pan Card Club Pvt Ltd. which included a retired Chairman of LIC. I knew his purpose of showing it to me but I was unmoved.

As expected, he came to me the next day. I handed over the letter of regret and said, "Mr Morvekar, your proposal cannot be accepted." He was shocked. He said, "Mr Sathe you are losing a substantial amount of LIC business in the process. Marathi people do not do business but a few like me who want to venture out are pulled down by people like you. Remember, you will find me a man of a few thousand crores in the next decade."

"Now coming to your question of how ₹65 will become ₹200 in three years, Mr Sathe, it's good that you are not in business. One doesn't have to think of this question. One has to ensure that three people pay you ₹100 each when this maturity amount of ₹200 is to be paid. This is the beauty of multi-level marketing." I said, Mr Morvekar, when the chain of 1-3-9-27 will break at some point all those in the last chain will lose their money. I know how such Ponzi schemes operate and that is precisely why I did not approve your proposal. You would have printed on the back of your deposit receipt, the LIC logo and policy terms depicting as if the maturity amount is guaranteed by LIC, and when your chain would have broken, all those thousands and lakhs of depositors would have come to the LIC office demanding money." He left with a sullen face but not before saying, "Mr Sathe, you will regret rejecting my proposal."

Many years passed and in 2014 when I was CEO of LIC Nomura Mutual Fund, I noticed a piece of news scrolling on TV about Pan Card Club. I became alert and eager to watch the news coverage. It showed a picture of thousands of depositors assembled at the Club's Mahim office demanding their deposit refund. One lady was lamenting that the maturity cheque was dishonoured. Another old person was complaining that he lost over a few lakhs of his hard-earned money. He got carried away by the fake promise of doubling his money in three years and lost everything. The reporter was saying "Mr Morvekar has absconded and left the country with over ₹7,000 crore and lakhs of depositors were being cheated...". Later I came to know that he died in the US.

After seeing that news, I patted myself on my back for the right decision I took in 1999-2000. It also came to my mind that so long as people get lured by higher interest rates, they will continue to lose their money in such Ponzi schemes. More and more Morvekars will cheat them. But I had the satisfaction of saving my organisation from the possible vilification and defamation.

In the year 2000-2001, the insurance sector was opened for Private/Foreign players. LIC's monopoly in the insurance sector came to an end. Many officers, Branch Managers, Senior Divisional Managers (SDMs) got lured away by the high salaries offered to them and left LIC to join private insurance companies. Suddenly, the SDM of Mumbai DO-IV tendered his resignation and I was selected in his place to head the division as DM in charge. It was a great opportunity for me to head a division and show my marketing acumen as the work involved was to increase insurance business and improve policy servicing in 18 Branches in the Fort area. I was allotted a car and residential telephone since I, once again, moved to the marketing side.

It was a difficult time for us at LIC as the private insurance companies had started their operations and were offering very high packages to experienced and competent marketing officials of LIC. Many officers were lured with these lucrative offers and submitted their resignations. Those who left LIC were really good officers. It was a great challenge for me to keep the morale of the good marketing officials high and to keep them motivated to increase business. I was able to manage the situation well and arrested the exodus of officers from my division. I developed an excellent rapport with the Development Officers (DOs) and Agents, kept them on their toes and at the same time brought about improvement in working of the Branches and thereby ensured ease of doing business for the marketing force. All my efforts yielded results and during the financial year 2000-2001 out of the four divisions in Mumbai, only our Division, Mumbai DO-IV, achieved its business targets.

My promotion was due. My performance in the P&GS Department Central office for three years and as DM in charge of Mumbai DO-IV for a year was noteworthy but so long as one's name is not in the promotion list, there is no guarantee of it. Fortunately, I was promoted as Senior DM and was posted in the same division as I had completed just a year in the division. The next year posed a bigger challenge for me, as I had to show a better performance over the earlier year's excellent results. I started adopting new concepts in marketing. I used to address meetings of groups of Agents attached to different DOs where I used to motivate them to scale newer heights. My emphasis to them was, "Don't ignore a client because he is paying a small premium or sum assured policy, remember that as his business grows, he will come to you to purchase more policies in the future. A pawn in chess may move only one square at a time. But when it reaches the last square, it can become a queen. A pawn should not be ignored, as it has the potential of becoming a queen."

In such meetings, I talked about handling objections raised by the prospects about buying insurance and also explained to the Agents how to convince their prospects to buy insurance. One common excuse was 'not today, I will buy it some other day'. I used to tell them a story from Mahabharat where once a mendicant came to Yudhishthir's door requesting for alms. As Yudhishthir was busy worshipping God he said, "Please come tomorrow". On hearing this, Bhim who was around started beating drums and when Yudhishthir asked him the reason for the same, he said, "My dear brother, I am delighted to know that you will be alive for one more day since you have asked the mendicant to come tomorrow. When no one can predict if he will be alive the next moment, my brother can; hence I am beating the drum in joy." Yudhishthir realised his mistake, went out, called the mendicant back and gave him alms.

Nobody can predict 'tomorrow'. If you have money today, buy insurance today. I used to explain to them by giving examples from old epics like Ramayan, Mahabharat, compositions of saints like Tukaram, Ramdas and some examples from day to day lives. I was told by some marketing officials that their Agents didn't attend meetings called by them. I used to tell them, "You should give them inputs which they don't have, make the topic interesting and non-repetitive and never ask for business. After the meeting, they themselves should get enthused and excited to do insurance business."

In order to provide a readymade solution to the prospects' likely objections, we published a booklet titled *50 Objections and How to Meet Them*. It contained objections like:

- I am still a bachelor. I don't need insurance.
- I don't have enough money to set aside for insurance.
- My brother is an Agent. Why should I buy it from you?
- Why should I buy it from LIC when I have a choice to buy it from private insurance companies?
- My income is below the taxable limit. It doesn't benefit me.

In some meetings, I used to have mock trials in which I used to make a smart LIC Agent a client and I used to pose as an Agent. He would raise an objection and I would convince him. This mock trial used to be quite interesting. In one such mock trial the client said, "My brother himself is an LIC Agent."

"Oh! That's good but I am wondering why he has not given you insurance yet. There may be two reasons. Either he doesn't think that you are worth buying insurance or you don't want to buy it from him because we need income proof before giving insurance which you may not be willing to share with your brother."

"Understand the client's psychology and talk accordingly." Those days a lakh or two was a big amount. Instead of asking the client to take insurance of a sum assured of ₹3 lakh, if you ask him, "Can you set aside ₹50 per day?" He may quickly agree and then give him an endowment policy with a sum assured of ₹3 lakh.

My efforts yielded results. It was for the first time, after many years of formation of Mumbai DO-IV, that our division surpassed the business of Mumbai DO-I on premium and sum assured, which was a record. Just after the business figures were out, the SDM of Mumbai DO-I submitted his papers as he wanted to join a private insurance company on a hefty pay packet. He was consecutively the third SDM of Mumbai DO-I, who put in his papers to join a private insurance company. It was not a good sign as MDO I was the Division which existed since LIC was formed. It had strong Union base, indisciplined employees, and on top of it, as the last three SDMs had decided to quit LIC, they might not have made any efforts to set things right.

In the meanwhile, I had completed five years in Mumbai, the longest tenure compared to any other city I was posted in previously. I knew that after being in charge of a Division for two years, I would be transferred. I, indeed, got transferred, but not out of Mumbai, I was posted as SDM of MDO I. It was a pleasant surprise for all of us. Since both the Divisions were in the same Yogakshema building, I had just to move from a cabin on the second floor to a cabin on the third floor. After a grand farewell by the agents, DOs and employees, I joined MDO I in May 2002.

During my days in MDO IV, I had great satisfaction in helping customers in distress by taking certain steps and finding certain solutions which can never be found in any text book. You need to think out of the box and walk the extra mile to help the customers.

One day, a customer in his mid-sixties, came to me almost in tears saying that he had lost about ₹1800 simply because of his carelessness. As a last resort he had come to me to request if I might help him. He had come to the LIC Branch to pay a quarterly premium in cash about three months ago and had brought his policy number written on a piece of paper, which he gave to the cashier. Either the policy number written by him was wrong or the number entered by the cashier in the computer was wrong, as a result of it the premium receipt issued was in some other name. Without checking the name on the receipt, he carried it home in a hurry only to realise three months later when a reminder for the last quarterly premium was received by him a day before.

I saw the receipt and the premium reminder notice and observed that there was variation of only one digit in both the policy numbers, while the premium was almost the same. I also noticed that the person in whose name the premium payment was wrongly adjusted was the District & Sessions judge in Aurangabad. I assured him that I would help him. I took his phone number and asked him to come after a few days.

I contacted the SDM Aurangabad and requested him to send me the residential telephone number of the judge whose name was mentioned on the receipt. He promptly helped me with the telephone number.

In the evening on reaching home, I made a phone call to the judge, introduced myself and briefly explained to him the reason for my call. The judge was very polite and responsive. He said, "When I sent my person to pay the last quarterly premium at the LIC Branch, I was told that the premium was already paid. I was worried as to who might have paid my premium. The mystery is solved. Now please tell me what I should do?" I took down his fax number and told him, "I shall fax you your premium receipt paid by the person in Mumbai erroneously and his premium notice and requested him to pay the premium of the person in Mumbai, as the amount was almost the same." He agreed to do so.

The next day he paid the premium and faxed me the receipt which I then gave to the customer, whose glowing face and sense of gratitude, I can never forget. I always believed and used to tell the staff that it is the customer who pays us our salary and we should always take pleasure in helping him at all times. Empathise with the customer and you will come up with a solution to his problem, which may sometimes be an out of the box solution. What you get by walking an extra mile is great satisfaction coupled with tonnes of blessings.

Mumbai DO-I was an old division, with a strong Union base and notorious employees. It had sixteen Branches, over seven hundred employees, over three hundred DOs and over one-fifty officers.

After taking charge, I called a meeting of Branch Managers, some of whom I knew but I wanted to know their strengths and weaknesses. I studied their performance for the last three years, their leave record, their academic background etc. before I met them. I noticed that there was one SBM, Mr Shah, a Gujarati gentleman who had taken leave for over a month during the busy days of March closing. After the meeting of all Branch heads, I called him to my cabin and asked him the reason for his leave. In his own words, "Sir, please transfer me from Branch 883 and if you won't, I may be murdered one day or I may commit suicide." I became alert and said, "Mr Shah, why are you so desperate to get transferred? It's a small Branch on the ground floor of Yogakshema. You are over fifty-six years old, you continue there for a year and next year I will transfer you to a bigger Branch where you may continue for two to three years till your retirement. But before I decide, whether to continue you or to transfer you please tell me why did you take leave for over a month during the busy days of closing in the last financial year, 2001-02 and what are you so terribly afraid of?" I could see the tension on his face when he said,

"Sir, a senior Assistant, Mrs Paramjit Kaur is responsible for my leave. She is simply a terror. She cannot be handled by me. She has not used her pen for office work for the last ten to twelve years. Despite knowing this, I made a mistake in my life. It was the third week of March. Since many proposals for new business were pending, I called her in my cabin one day and requested her to scrutinise the proposals. I requested her politely to work at least in March. Hearing this, she became wild. She took out her *katyar* (dagger or a small sword) and said, "If you dare to ask me to work again, this sword will pass through your neck." I got scared, my BP shot up, I had to take rest for a month." I understood then that Mr Shah is so timid that even if he is given a pistol, he won't pull the trigger. I decided to shift him to some other Branch for which I asked him to submit a request. I also decided to post a daredevil, fearless Branch Manager to 883 Branch to teach Mrs Paramjit Kaur a lesson. Fortunately, in the inter-zonal transfers, an officer named Mr Dinesh Salathia, a young Punjabi officer was allotted to my Division on promotion as Branch Manager. I posted him to the 883 Branch and transferred Mr Shah to the 905 Branch.

During my first meeting with Mr Salathia, I asked him if he had met the staff after joining and asked him for his general impression of the Branch. He told me that except Mrs Kaur, the employees were all working to their best capacity. On his own he said, "Sir, if you permit, I would like to initiate disciplinary action against Mrs Kaur." I was happy that my choice was correct. I supported him and said, "I am on the same page as you. I want you to build a record against her to help me initiate action against her as I am the disciplinary authority for Assistants, under staff regulations." I noticed the confidence in his eyes. He said, "Sir, I will do the needful. I will shortly submit documentary evidence to enable you to take action."

Just after a month or so, he came to me at the close of office hours. He had brought with him evidence of Mrs Kaur being absent from office for almost half a day post lunch. When the officer to whom she was reporting asked her about her absence, she said, "I had gone to Central office. I don't have time to clarify further as I will miss my local train at 5:45 pm, so do whatever you want to do."

Dinesh had brought with him the necessary documentary evidence duly witnessed by two staff members. I called the concerned officers and the staff members to ascertain and to confirm the facts. I also got confirmation from them that they would fearlessly depose during the enquiry proceedings.

I issued her a Show Cause Notice (SCN) and on getting her reply I instituted an enquiry. No Union supported her. I imposed a penalty of two decrements which was certainly more severe than her misconduct of being absent for half a day. But I imposed a severe penalty initially so that if the Appellate Authority wanted to take a lenient view, it had scope to reduce the penalty to one decrement.

As expected, she appealed against the penalty to Zonal Manager, Mr T K Banerjee. Before disposing of her appeal, one day Mr Banerjee called me and said, "Mr Sathe, you have imposed a severe penalty which is disproportionate to her misconduct."

"Sir, yes I agree but you may ask anyone from the Branch if the lady has done any LIC work in the last ten years. Even the unions have not come to her rescue."

"Mr Sathe, what you say may be correct but is it on record? None of your predecessors have ever issued her a letter even calling for an explanation. Being an Appellate Authority, I have decided only to censure her (a very mild penalty which is like a warning in normal parlance).

I was upset. I tried to convince him to reduce the penalty to one decrement but he was unmoved. Finally I said "Sir, if I continue to initiate action against her, I hope that you won't reduce the penalty imposed by me in future." The smile on his face was his confirmation. During the next two years I issued her Show Cause Notices for indiscipline, one after the other and brought her to the minimum pay scale of Assistants. Mr Banerjee, ZM also upheld the penalties imposed by me on her appeal. The last Show Cause notice for which I had instituted an enquiry was un-concluded when I left the Division on promotion in 2003.

Many a time we hide our incompetence under the garb of bosses, saying that they won't support us. But if the disciplinary proceedings are properly conducted, it becomes difficult for the appellate authority to reverse it. We need to be bold and should have the basic knowledge of the laws of the land. I had appointed lady officers as the Enquiry Officer and the Presenting Officer. I gave enough time to Ms Kaur to reply to the SCN. Principle of natural justice was always followed. The enquiries were conducted in a flawless manner as it should always be.

There is a general perception that in the public sector indiscipline is tolerated, nobody bothers, bosses are afraid to take disciplinary action as the unions are strong. Of course, it is not totally unfounded. I have seen a few senior officers saying, "I don't want you to bring to my notice that Mr ABC of your Branch doesn't work. Think as if he is not posted to your Branch. I have made equitable distribution of all such non-performing assets (NPAs) and you have no reason to grumble." I was one who never tolerated indiscipline. I was always fearless in communicating to the employees that no nonsense would be tolerated.

I used to get a consolidated statement every month about employees from the Branches and the Division who were on 'unauthorised absence'. Soon after taking charge of the division I noticed that one Assistant, Mr Rajeev Rane of 929 Branch, was on unauthorised absence for over ten months. Personnel department informed me that the Branch was writing him letters but there was no response from the employee. I called Mr Nandkumar Ghonge, DM (Personnel) and asked him, "See Mr Ghonge, this employee is not reporting to duty for the last ten months, can anyone survive in Mumbai without getting a salary? Why didn't you direct the

Branch to send someone to his residential address to ascertain if he is alive or dead? Who knows, he may be in difficulty and may be in need of help. Before coming to office tomorrow, you yourself go to his residence, meet him and only then come to office." He agreed. The next day he reached office with a smile on his face and said, "Sir, outside his residence, in Government Colony Bandra, I saw a board 'Adv. Rajeev Rane'. I became alert and went to his office posing as if I had come to seek his advice in some legal matter. He was not there but a lady who was sitting in his office gave me his visiting card and advised me to contact him after 4:00 pm as he had gone to the court." He gave me that visiting card. I asked him to initiate action against him. I also told him that had he done it before it would have been better, to which he agreed.

A letter was sent to Rajeev Rane stating "It has come to our notice that in spite of the fact that you are on the rolls of LIC Branch 929 as Assistant, you are found practising in court. Please explain within fifteen days, why action should not be initiated against you..."

I knew that for getting a certificate of practice as a lawyer, one has to apply to the Bar Council and in the application had he written 'Employed with LIC' against the question 'Are you employed?' no Bar Council would have issued him a certificate of practice. So, I guessed he must have written 'No' against the question about 'Present employment'. If we could get a copy of the said application, it would be easy for us to prove our charges.

Our department wrote to the Secretary, Bar Council of Mumbai, a couple of times but I was told that there was no response. My friend Mr S K Roy (who later became Chairman LIC) was Secretary (Legal) then. One day I told him about the case and requested him to help me in getting an appointment with the Secretary, Bar Council of Mumbai. He knew one contact through whom Mr Ghonge met the Secretary of the Bar Council and managed to get a certified copy of Mr Rajeev Rane's 'Application to practice in court'.

It was clear from the application that Mr Rane had lied that he was not employed anywhere. Based on it, we wrote to the Bar Council to cancel his Certificate of Practice as he was in employment with LIC. Simultaneously a show-cause notice was issued to him and later an enquiry was instituted against him. He appeared on the date of enquiry and held my feet and started crying. I called Mr Ghonge. In front of him, he started narrating his story.

"Sir, I am from a poor family in Konkan (coastal area of Maharashtra). I was the first in our family to get a graduation degree. I have a younger brother and a sister. My father lost his job in the cotton mill. I secured a job in LIC Mumbai and had to send most of my salary to my father. I knew that the money I sent was always inadequate for my parents, hence I enrolled myself for LLB and completed the course in three years. My friend advised me to start practice and if the earnings, in a year, crossed income from salary, to resign from LIC and continue as a lawyer while if I don't make enough in practice, I may join the job in LIC again. Sir, you have since taken up the matter with the Bar Council, I will be debarred from practice as a lawyer and I will lose my LIC job as well. I will be on the streets. Please forgive me. Fortunately, I am doing well as a lawyer. Please accept my resignation and do not follow up with the Bar Council." I consulted Mr Ghonge and on his advice asked Mr Rane to submit his resignation forthwith, deposit one month's salary in lieu of notice period which he did promptly and I let him go. Did I do anything wrong? I think his intention was good but the path he chose would have left him with no choice in the near future except face ruin. I taught him a lesson but gave him a lease of life. One should enforce discipline but should generally not be ruthless and lose compassion.

It was in 2003 when I was senior Divisional Manager of Mumbai DO. 1, I was *'gheraoed'* by one of the aggressive nationalist unions. I could tactfully and fearlessly face the *'gherao'*. It so happened that LIC employees were entitled for Leave Travel Concession (LTC) to visit any place in India with family once in two years and claim reimbursement of II AC Railway tickets. One active member of the union was reported to have claimed the reimbursement without actually travelling by train. I called him and asked him if what I heard was true. He said, "Sir, I have already got reimbursement, now do what you want to do." Had he accepted his untruthfulness, I would have asked him to pay back the money he received on account of the false claim and might have forgiven him. But even after giving him a chance to correct himself, he remained adamant. I called the concerned officer and asked him to write to the railway office to check if anybody had travelled on those tickets or if the reserved tickets were later cancelled. Within eight to ten days, we got a letter from the railway office stating that those reserved tickets were later cancelled. I issued him a Show Cause notice enclosing the evidence and asking as to why disciplinary proceedings should not be initiated against him. On getting the Show Cause Notice (SCN), he read the writing on the wall. The charges could easily be proved and once misappropriation is established, he could have even been terminated. He immediately approached the union leaders and the next day, a mob of twenty to twenty-five employees, some known but most of them were unfamiliar (may not be from LIC, how does one know?) entered my cabin without notice. The leader, in a loud and arrogant tone said, "He is our member. You cannot take action against him. You take back the SCN and close the matter."

"That won't happen. He has misappropriated the amount and will be punished."

"We won't leave your cabin unless you withdraw the SCN. Consider it as our '*gherao*'."

I called the sub staff and said, "Shyam, the union wants to *gherao* me. You close the door of my cabin from outside. If I am not allowed to leave my seat, nobody else can leave my cabin either."

He bolted the cabin from outside. After their initial slogan shouting, the leader again said, "You take back SCN." I said in a loud voice, "Is he not ashamed of claiming bogus LTC? It's widows' money. Had it been given by me from my pocket, I would have written it off. But I am a custodian of policyholders' money and I will not spare him. Railway authorities have confirmed that the reservations were cancelled. He will have to face the enquiry. I won't take back the SCN. I don't mind if you don't lift the *gherao*."

Hearing my loud voice, his voice toned down. He said, "Sir, forgive and forget." I said, "Sorry. Not possible." They probably never expected me to be so unrelenting. After sometime, another leader in a soft tone said, "Sir, I agree he did wrong but be large hearted and give him a soft punishment." I said, "That is what I may consider if the enquiry officer so suggests." They heaved a sigh of relief. Another fellow said, "Sir, we have *gheraoed* many officers in the past but this is the first *gherao* where the voice of the *'gheraoed'* person was louder than ours. Sir, we are lifting the *gherao* but please treat him with compassion." I did not give them any assurance and signalled Shyam to open the door. As they saw that the door of the cabin was unlocked, one by one, they left. Their leader who was so arrogant in the beginning had toned down his voice and shook hands with me with a request not to tell other unions about the failed *gherao*. I laughed.

Later the employee, in his reply to SCN, accepted the charges. Charges could be easily proved in the enquiry proceedings, but by that time, the employee had mellowed down. He paid back the amount wrongly claimed by him. I took a soft stand and did not remove him from service but imposed a penalty of four decrements.

In another case of an employee, however, I had to be ruthless. There was a Senior Assistant, Mrs Sapatnekar, who for some reason or the other had become totally insane. She used to come to office at her own sweet will, badly dressed, her clothes would stink, used to move around whistling. It appeared as if she had not taken a bath not just for a day or two but for weeks together. She was in this mental condition for the last over ten years and had at least ten more years of service left. One day two lady employees who were sitting on both sides of the table where Mrs Sapatnekar used to sit, came to me complaining about her and said, "Sir such a foul smell is coming from her clothes that it is just impossible to sit next to her. Please change our seats. We are feeling nauseous." I immediately called Manager (Office Services) and asked him to move Mrs Sapatnekar's table next to Mr Mukund Damle, who was a union leader and was on leave then. The two lady Assistants thanked me profusely. After a couple of days, Mr Damle joined the office and came to me running, holding a handkerchief on his nose and said "Sir! It appears that you don't want me to sit in the office. The foul smell emanating from Mrs Sapatnekar is preventing me from sitting next to her even for a minute."

I said, "Mr Damle, for the last ten years some employee or the other seated next to her suffered, now it's your turn."

Mr Damle said, "Sir, we have tried to tell her many times to take a bath before coming to office but in vain. It's high time that we remove her from service."

I asked him to get her residential phone number as I wanted to talk to her husband and try and see if she would resign. The next day Mr Damle came to me with her residential phone number and I connected the call. Mr Sapatnekar, was on the line. I put the call on speaker to let Mr Damle hear what the conversation was. When I told him about her untidy clothes, stinking smell etc. he said, "Mr Sathe, I am surprised how your organisation is tolerating her for so many years. She is unbearable even for us. She has gone totally insane. I won't be able to convince her to resign. You take action, whatever you deem fit."

That solved my problem. It was easy to take action against her as she never used to report on time and rarely used to be on her seat. I issued her charge sheets, one after the other, no union leader including Mr Damle came to her defence and finally within nine to ten months I terminated her. She was so out of her mind that she did not even submit an appeal. Even after her termination, she continued to come to office but was prevented by security staff from entering the premises. She still used to come, sit on the stairs at the entrance, would keep whistling and after some time she would leave. After some days, she stopped coming to the office. Many lady employees thanked me for my action.

Thoughts such as, 'What way am I concerned? If my predecessors did not take action why should I? Her salary is not going from my pocket. It is an insignificant pay-out for LIC. Why should I give a case to the union and invite wrath?', never crossed my mind while doing my duty.

By 2001, at least six private insurance companies had started their operations. In a short time, their presence was being felt. Their Branch offices were neat and clean with cubicles and air-conditioning. As against their offices, our offices were too big to manage. The record rooms were scary to enter being full of dust, old ceiling fans used to dangle and make ghostly noise which was heard even in the noisy atmosphere of the Branch. There were old tables of different sizes laid out without any care for décor, furniture of different shapes, sizes and colour was a normal scene in a Branch. Staff members of the private insurance companies were smartly dressed and spoke fluent English. The salary offered to these well-dressed employees was twice or thrice the salary paid to the well-experienced staff of LIC. In this backdrop, it was a big challenge for LIC to be the 'Most preferred insurance company'.

LIC management quickly realised the need for change and the board approved modernisation of Branches starting with metro Branches. In the first hundred Branches to be modernised, six Branches from Mumbai DO-I were chosen. With modernisation of Branches, the Branches would have cubicles, air-conditioning, compactors for dockets filing, underground cabling etc. It was also expected that the Branches would need less space resulting in surrender of at least twenty-five per cent of the Branch space.

'Oppose the change' being the mentality of the unions, I received a letter signed by office bearers of all the unions raising their objection on various aspects of the modernisation proposal and the most important being reduction in area per employee.

I called them for discussion, showed them the designs and drawings, alerted them of the need to modernise in the era of competition, addressed Town Hall meetings of employees of all the six Branches which were to be modernised. I used to show them a slide of a famous actress with a distorted face and ask them to identify her. While they were discussing among themselves as to who the actress was, I would show them on the next slide, a proper beautiful picture of the actress saying, "The first picture is of your present Branch and the next one is of your modernised Branch. In general, the staff members were happy with the proposal but routinely used to raise objections like 'during office hours if the work is carried out, the dust may impact our health.' I used to tell the contractor in front of them not to carry out work during office hours and to keep the Branch clean before 9:00 am in the morning. I used to ask him about the time he would take to complete the work. I knew that the time given was sixty days but on getting this reply from him, I would assure the employees that they would be happy to work in a 'posh' Branch after seventy-five days.

After convincing the employees and their unions, the actual work of modernisation started. I provided masks to all employees as a safeguard against dust. I was keeping a close watch to ensure that no casualty occurs but still in one Branch a ceiling fan came down with a thud. Fortunately, nobody was injured. I ensured a daily visit to all those Branches where modernisation work had started.

One should not only be concerned for the welfare of employees but should also be 'seen' to be concerned. I ensured that I was 'seen concerned' as well. It was not a show off but my heartfelt concern.

Despite all this when I had gone to 931 Branch to see the progress of work, I was *gheraoed* by fourteen or fifteen Development Officers demanding three visitors' chairs for every DO instead of two. In the process, obviously the area per DO would have increased but if I had accepted their demand, a similar demand would have been raised by the DOs of other Branches as well. Hence I had to be tactical in dealing with them. I tried to convince them but they were not ready to relent. Finally, I called the union representatives of Class I and Class III unions and told them, "I cannot continue modernisation of your Branch because of your DO friends who don't want modernisation." They said in one voice, "Who says that we don't want modernisation? If the DO friends do not want it, let them continue with the old set-up." I called the contractor and asked him that no air-conditioners be fixed in the DO wing and the Branch modernisation should be done as planned except for the areas which were occupied by the DOs.

The DOs never expected me to take such a stand. They could foresee that they had to be in the old set-up without air-conditioning when the rest of the Branch would have a beautiful look.

I followed the management theory, 'Listen to all, announce your decision and leave immediately without lingering around'.

The next day, two office bearers of the DO Union of Branch 931 came to meet me and apologised for their stand. I asked them to submit a letter to me, signed by all the DOs if the modernization work of DO wing was to resume. They did it and the Branch got modernised as per the plan and time schedule.

I had to take a tougher stand in Branch 914. After about a month of starting the work, when it was time to remove the tables of DOs, the Senior Branch Manager (SBM) reported to me that the DOs were hell bent on not allowing the tables to be removed. I went to the Branch, asked the DOs in a meeting, "Why did you not object to modernisation right in the beginning? Now when the cubicles are ready to be fitted, your objection is unfounded. Your tables will be removed today evening. Ensure that all the drawers are empty. The tables will be shifted to the godown tonight and the management won't be responsible for the loss of any papers or belongings in the drawer."

A senior DO said, "Even if our tables are removed, we won't allow the cubicles to be fitted there." They might have thought that I would buckle under their arrogance but I called the contractor and instructed him to shift the tables and chairs on 'as is where is' basis to the godown by 6:00 pm. I asked him not to start the work of fitting the cubicles and asked the SBM to hire cotton carpets and spread those in the area from where the tables were removed. He did as was instructed.

The next day when the DOs came, they found their tables missing. They went to the SBM asking about the alternate seating arrangement to which he replied, "The Indian way of sitting on the floor is arranged for you, please sit on the cotton carpet and do your work." The DOs refused to sit on the floor and gave a 'No Business Call'. I knew that they would use pressure tactics to pressurise me but I also knew that their Agents won't support them for long. It was an 'undeclared Strike'. They went on mass casual leave. I knew that they couldn't afford to continue it for long. After four days, a few performing DOs started coming to the Branch and on the sixth day, they came to meet me. "Sir, we are put to a great lot of inconvenience in the last few days. Our Agents are blaming us for the deadlock. Please get the work restarted and get us the cubicles as soon as possible." I called the contractor and instructed him to finish the work of modernization of Branch 914 quickly. One after the other, in just three months of commencement of work, all six Branches became fully functional with a 'modern look'. Next year, all the other Branches of the division got modernised with almost no resistance from the employees.

In LIC, the post of Sr DM in charge gives you a lot of experience in 'problem solving' and 'counselling'. You become an expert in 'fire-fighting'. You come across some problem for which you won't find a solution in any management course.

One day, Mr Vikas Jagdhari, BM of 929 Branch came to me with one such problem. He looked quite tense and said, "Sir, our Branch is banking with Standard Chartered Bank which is just opposite our Branch. While reconciling the bank account for the month of February 2004 it was noticed that a cheque for

₹1 lakh issued in favour of a policyholder was actually debited by the bank for ₹10 lakh. I rushed to the bank without further delay to get a photocopy of the cheque. The cheque appeared to have been altered from ₹1 lakh to ₹10 lakh but has been properly signed by the authorised signatories at every alteration. The officers who had signed the cheque claim that they had issued the cheque for ₹1 lakh only without any alterations and the signatures on the altered amount in words and figures appear to be forged. It's a clear case of fraud. I have rushed to you to seek your advice and guidance on the matter."

I looked at the photocopy of the cheque minutely. My experience of working in a bank for five years helped me notice that although the corrections were duly signed at two places, but 'not exceeding ₹1,00,000' was not altered to '₹10,00,000'. The person who might have forged the signatures appeared to have missed it. The officer of Standard Chartered Bank who passed the cheque appeared to have missed the above point. Had he noticed it, he would have certainly dishonoured the cheque.

I spoke with the Branch Manager of the bank and asked him to come to meet me urgently. He soon came along with one more officer of the bank. I showed him a copy of the cheque and asked him to reverse the entry. I said, "A fraudulently altered cheque has been debited to our account without ensuring that the corrections are carried out at all the places. I pointed out to him that 'Not over ₹1,00,000 has not been altered to ₹10,00,000'. A suspicion should have arisen in the mind of the passing officer and he should have dishonoured the cheque. It is a gross mistake of the bank and as such the entry should be reversed."

To this, he argued "Sir, the signatures on alterations appear to be identical, as if made by the authorised signatories of LIC. Fraud appears to have been committed by the LIC Branch staff."

"I will investigate."

"Bank will take action only after the investigation is carried out."

"Sorry, gentleman, our internal investigation has nothing to do with your wrong debit to our account. You reverse the entry first."

The Bank Manager was unwilling to do so.

He requested me to give him one week's time to conduct a forensic audit and then to take further course of action. It was 15 March, I wanted to close the issue before 31 March 2004 but still I gave him one week's time. I told him that if I won't hear from him by 22 March I would proceed with filing a Police complaint and initiating legal action. Before leaving, the other bank officer said, "Sir, when the cheque is doubtful, we send a copy of the cheque by fax to the customer to get confirmation but your Branch has no fax machine. I had spoken to some officer of LIC Branch that due to this cheque, your account is getting overdrawn and only after receiving instructions from LIC to transfer ₹10 lakh from another bank account which had enough balance, did we pass the cheque. We had thus taken adequate care."

I asked, "Why did you allow LIC Branch to open their bank account with you when having a fax machine was your pre-requisite for opening an account? Did the LIC office mention that they have a fax machine while opening the account? LIC Branch is exactly opposite to your bank. You could have sent a person to LIC to get confirmation. If we notice that one bank account has insufficient balance, we transfer the required amount from another account and this practice is followed to ensure that no LIC cheque gets dishonoured." He had no further arguments.

Vikas Jagdhari went to the Branch. He showed the cheque to both the officers who had signed the cheque as authorised signatories. Both the officers had an excellent track record and he concluded that they had no involvement in the fraud.

The Bank Manager in due course informed me of his inability to reverse the entry. Then I suggested to him that we should jointly file a Police complaint so that the fraudster could be caught. He consulted the bank's solicitors and came back to me informing that the bank was not interested in filing an FIR. I expressed my displeasure and told him, "In which case, I will have no choice but to implead your bank in the case mentioning that some employees of your bank, in connivance with some unknown persons have defrauded LIC. Our solicitors have given me a draft of an FIR to be filed with the Police. It's already 25 March 2004. I can't wait anymore. If you don't come back to me within the next twenty-four hours, I will be constrained to file an FIR with Police mentioning possible involvement of your bank staff in the fraud."

This threat yielded results. The next day he called up and said, "Sir, I am sending you a letter stating that the entry will be reversed before 31 March 2004. Please do not implicate our bank or its employees in the FIR."

I got the letter and accordingly the bank reversed the entry on 31 March 2004 without a reminder from our end.

The next week, the Bank Manager came to me with a request to close the LIC Br 929 account with them. As it is, we too were not comfortable dealing with the foreign bank. Before he left, I asked him the reason why he didn't join me in filing an FIR to which he said, "Sir, ours is a foreign bank. We do not want our bank's name to appear in the newspapers saying that the bank is defrauded. We have hence raised a debit as, 'Amounts due from employees' to the extent of ₹10 lakh. This amount will be recovered from all the employees involved in passing the cheque."

I understood why these foreign banks pay such hefty salaries to their employees. I was happy that I could save LIC of loss of ₹10 lakh with my prompt and tactful action.

I always believed that manuals, rule books, guidance notes are not sacrosanct. They are helpful while taking decisions but they should not be brought under the category of a 'Holy Book'. If manuals are to be followed in toto without an exception, robots should be employed and not human beings. If your conscience is clear and the purpose is honest, one should not worry about making an exception to the rule. I made it once and I got a treasure in my life in the form of the lovable Heranjal family.

One day our senior Agent, Mrs Anusuya Heranjal came to me. She was accompanied by her husband who was holding a white cane which indicated that he was visually impaired. I made them sit comfortably. I had not met her before. From the visiting card which she had sent to me before entering my cabin, I could find that she was a high performing LIC Agent and was awarded the prestigious Chairman's Club Membership by LIC. I offered them a glass of water and asked the sub staff to get us some good coffee. Then I asked her the reason for her visit. She looked upset. She said, "Sir, I am thankful to LIC for helping me with income when I needed it most. But now, after being an Agent for over twenty-five years and after crossing the age of sixty, unfortunately the time has come for me to leave this noble work. LIC has given me money, self-respect, and a position in society. However, for no fault of mine, since LIC has decided to withdraw my Chairman's Club Membership, I have decided to stop working for LIC as an Agent and she showed me a letter received by her which stated, "Since you could not complete the minimum level of new business during last year required for continuation of your club membership, the same stands withdrawn. You are, as such, not entitled to any benefits available to the Chairman's Club."

Let me explain what is so great about the Club Membership in LIC. Depending on consistent new business performance for the last five years, based on their level of performance, Agents are awarded membership of BM/DM/ZM/CM Club (LIC has now added two more clubs beyond the Chairman's Club). The Chairman's Club (CM) membership is difficult to get and still more difficult to continue because if for any reason, you fail to bring in the requisite new business in a financial year, you have to do the requisite business for four years again to acquire the lost Club Membership. Nobody hence wants to lose club membership and a host of its benefits like housing loans at quite a cheap rate of interest, office allowance, interest-free car loan, festival advance, free group Insurance, facility to attend the annual convention in big cities for which air travel is allowed, etc. More than the monetary benefits, it provides prestige as less than two per cent Agents are club members.

Anyone would have been disheartened to lose the prestigious club's membership but I wanted to know why she could not do the requisite new business last year which led to the loss of her club membership. By then, she had relaxed. She opened up about her life to me.

"Except for the three to four months during the last financial year when I was bed-ridden, I was in good health and was enthusiastically and wholeheartedly doing LIC agency. I wanted to avoid the addition of the word 'Ex' or 'Former' before my club membership and as such, now since LIC has terminated my club membership, I have decided to resign."

"Please tell me the reason for your ill-health last year?"

"Sir, I had a bypass surgery and was advised to rest for three months thereafter and it was during the peak months of business from December to March. I could, hence not complete the required business for continuation of my club membership. I think LIC has done injustice to me by overlooking the reason why I couldn't do the requisite business. It was due to my bypass surgery. I have come to you with an appeal for justice."

I knew that no exception was ever made in awarding or continuation of club membership in the past. I had not heard of any such case before. She showed me her medical history and the medical papers that she had brought. After going through the papers, I said, "You are going to live a hundred years since I see that your bypass surgery was done by the renowned heart surgeon, Dr Nitu Mandke. With a smile on her face she said, "Sir, if that is so, I should live past hundred as Dr Nitu Mandke has not charged me a penny for the surgery. He has done it absolutely free of cost despite our insistence."

When I asked her the reason for the same, she said, "Sir, I have three daughters and a son. Out of the four, three are super speciality doctors. The eldest Lata is a dermatologist, the next, Poornima is a gynaecologist and my son Shashikant is anaesthesiologist. One daughter is a PG settled in Dubai. Dr Nitu Mandke was a classmate of my daughter Poornima who has settled in the UK. During her exams, in order to save the travel time, she used to stay in the medical college hostel. I used to send her tiffin daily. We are *Karwaris*, well known fish-eaters. I used to send her a tiffin with a variety of fish dishes which she used to share with her friends, one of them was Dr Nitu Mandke. So, while declining to accept any fees from me for the surgery, he said, "Aai, I have already taken enough fees from you during my college days in the form of delicious fish curry, the taste of which still lingers on my tongue."

"Madam, you know that the road to the heart goes through the stomach!" I said, and she laughed.

As we were finishing our cup of coffee, I asked her how she became an LIC Agent. She said, "My husband who was working in the Bank of India, suddenly lost his eye-sight and had to leave the job. I was not even a matriculate then. Managing a family of six with school and college going children was a big issue. We had a neighbour Mr S B Deb, a DO of LIC who was a Bengali but spoke Marathi very well. He offered me the LIC agency. In those days, LIC agency was given even to those who were not matriculates. I had no experience in marketing, I knew no English, I was a semi-literate housewife, but Mr Deb assured me of all the help with form-filling etc. He taught me only a few plans of insurance and came with me initially to meet two to three prospects. As I got my first commission cheque, I became confident and then became an established LIC Agent. Mr Deb came to my rescue in the form of God (Deb/Deo in Marathi means God). Let me tell you honestly, I could pay for higher education for my children only because of the commission I earned from LIC and hence now, although I don't need money for my livelihood and even though my children keep coaxing me to stop LIC work, I tell them that LIC is like my mother. I would not have left the LIC agency till my death but with a heavy heart, now I have to leave the agency."

I consoled her. I took papers of her surgery, called the P.A. and asked her to type her representation for continuation of the Chairman's Club membership. I comforted her and said, "Don't get disheartened. Let me see if I can be of help to you."

Mr Heranjal who was patiently listening to the conversation, blessed me and said, "Mr Sathe, I have worked in a bank for many years but the empathy you have shown is seldom seen in senior officers. You have my blessings even if my wife's work is not done. I bless you. You will reach the pinnacle of glory and will be successful in your career."

My P.A. in the meanwhile, brought the representation, took her signature thereon and attached the medical reports to it. After it was done, I assured them that I would look into the matter.

The next day, I took an appointment with Mr S B Mathur, who was Chairman, LIC then. I briefly explained the case details to him and said, "Sir, I know that the rules do not permit any relaxation in this case. But I request you to consider this case on humanitarian grounds." I further told him that if he was to consider her appeal, only then would I forward it through the proper channel. Mr Mathur was a pragmatic leader. He said, "Mr Sathe, if you honestly think that I should consider her case, I will do so." I was happy. I met Mr T K Banerjee, Zonal Manager, the next day and requested him to forward it to the Central office. I also told him that the Chairman had assured me that he would consider it.

After about a week, I got a letter from the CO condoning the deficiency in business done by Mrs Heranjal and approving the continuation of her Chairman's Club membership. I called Mrs Heranjal on the phone and asked her to meet me the next day.

She used to take her husband along whenever she visited the LIC office just to avoid his loneliness and possible dejection. They would travel by train in the compartment reserved for disabled persons. She used to bring him so that he would not feel dejected and lonely at home. I showed her the letter received from the CO. She didn't know English and her husband was visual impaired, hence I read the letter aloud, the meaning of which Mr Heranjal explained to her in Konkani, their mother tongue, which resembles Marathi. Both of them were extremely delighted. Mr Heranjal profusely thanked me while Mrs Heranjal said, "Sir, you have given me a new lease of life. You have done something, which was impossible. I will now continue LIC agency work with vigour and I assure you that I won't give up my agency till my death."

We went on to develop a friendship between our families. We attended many of their family functions like the weddings of their grand-daughters etc. Whenever she came to Santacruz, she would bring fish or chicken curry for me as she knew that I liked to eat non-vegetarian food. She continued her agency even after her leg was amputated due to gangrene. She ensured that the word 'Ex' or 'Former' did not precede before her LIC agency.

During that time, I wrote an article on her in our house magazine, the gist of which was, "Don't call me grandma, I am as energetic as you. I want all of you to work hard and spread the message of insurance..." The purpose of the article was to motivate the young Agents. If such a semi-literate, old lady can continue her CM's Club membership by working hard, young Agents should follow her.

A 'Bucket list' is a 'to do list before you die. While a 'Reverse Bucket List' is a list of deeds which have given you immense satisfaction. Mrs Heranjal's case is on the top in my 'Reverse Bucket List.'

Although it is always said that one thing which is always constant is 'change' but nobody is ready to accept change, especially in the public sector. I had experienced it during modernisation of Branches. As if that experience was not enough, I was inducted into a committee of four, chaired by Mr Atul Shukla, ED (who later became Chairman LIC), to design a new Incentive Scheme for Development Officers (DOs). The then existing scheme of paying incentive bonus based on new business acquired by the Agents supervised by the DOs had outlived its purpose. It was not addressing the role of the DOs. It had lacunae due to which many DOs were getting huge incentives disproportionate to their efforts. Right in the beginning, Mr S B Mathur, Chairman, briefed the committee and said, "Imagine that you have started a new insurance company and you have to design a new scheme for assessing performance of DOs based on their functionalities and efforts. They should work to their full potential. They should promote the sale of such policies which LIC wants them to promote. They should not be dependent upon a few Agents. They should regularly keep recruiting Agents and their incentive should depend on efforts they make on developing, helping and mentoring Agents."

After the mandate was received, we started our work of identifying deficiencies of the existing scheme. We identified the reasons why and how the existing scheme was being misused. Many DOs were earning a huge amount of incentive bonus (which was over and above their salary) due to good business done by a few of their established Agents. They had stopped Agents recruitment activity. The DOs had no compulsion to be in office from 10:00 am to 5:00 pm. Some were reported to have started some shops of stationery, hosiery etc. Some were reported to be engaged in estate agency business. Some were reported to have taken agency of Japan Life (multi-level marketing company) while some were reported to be busy in some chit funds. Since the existing incentive scheme was purely based on the premium brought in by their Agents, once a few high performing Agents were under their belt, they were least bothered to look at the work that they were supposed to do. Many DOs were earning more than hundred times the salary of LIC Chairman. We were not against their earning incentives but we thought of aligning it to the efforts they put in to do business.

We drafted a scheme and named it, 'Growth Oriented Incentive Bonus Scheme (GOIB Scheme)'. We had a series of discussions with the DO Association and with the top management's Central Management Committee (CMC) and finally after it was cleared by the Chairman, it was placed before the Board which approved it. Salient features of the scheme on which the incentive would depend were:

- Every year a DO should recruit at least five Agents.
- He should have at least a few Agents bringing qualifying business of twenty lives in his appraisal year.
- He should ensure the sale of certain plans of insurance which LIC wanted to promote. It was observed that the DOs were promoting only a few plans of insurance which gave higher commission to the Agents and higher incentive to the DOs. As such, it was prescribed that a certain percentage of total sale should come from such 'focused plans'.
- The new scheme introduced a system of gradation of Agents based on their seniority. It's well known that a DO has to spend more time on identifying, recruiting, training and mentoring Agents in the initial years but as these Agents become professional, they do business on their own. Credit for business done by Agents above ten years was limited to forty per cent, between seven to ten years was limited to seventy-five per cent and for Agents below seven years it was kept at hundred per cent.

Again, the purpose of gradation was that they should focus on recruitment of Agents and get more business done from them. Many changes were suggested, some of them were accepted and finally on approval of the Board, it was implemented all over India.

The DOs obviously never wanted the then existing incentive bonus scheme to change. It was difficult for them to digest the new scheme. They staged demonstrations, gave 'no business call', burnt effigy of Mr Shukla, who was Chairman of the committee but the management did not budge to these pressure tactics. Working in a committee headed by Mr Atul Shukla, who was known for his analytical skills and fearless approach, was a great experience. Although we had to face a lot of discontent from our DO fraternity, we were happy that we did justice to the job assigned.

Lessons Learnt...

- Never argue with your Boss; you may win the argument but lose your promotion.
- So long as people get lured by higher interest rates, they will lose their money in Ponzi schemes.
- Don't disregard a client because he is paying a small premium. Remember, as his business grows, he will come to you to purchase more policies in future.
- A pawn in chess may move only one square at a time, but when it reaches the last square, it becomes a queen. Never ignore a pawn because it has the potential to become a queen.
- Nobody can predict 'tomorrow'. If you have money today, buy insurance today.
- It is the customer who pays us our salary. Empathise with him. Keep 'customer first' always in your mind. Think out of the box and walk an extra mile to help him.
- When disciplinary proceedings are properly conducted, it becomes difficult for the appellate authority to reverse it. You need to be bold and should have the basic knowledge of the law of the land.
- Listen to all, announce your decision and leave immediately without lingering around.
- Manuals, Rule Books, Guidance Notes are not sacrosanct; don't put them in the category of a 'Holy Book'. If your conscience is clear and the purpose is honest, one should not worry about making an exception to the rule.
- One should not only be concerned for the welfare of employees but should also be 'seen' to be concerned.

VII

Duty First

During those days, I used to commute from Jeevan Shanti Colony, Santacruz, to Yogakshema Building, Nariman Point, by car. We had a car pool with two of my colleagues, Mr Vinay Sah and Mr Rajeev Chaturvedi. It used to save fuel cost and also one had to drive his car only for two days in a week. It reduced the monotony of driving. It used to be great fun travelling together. Rajeev had a melodious voice and Vinay remembered old songs. I was a good storyteller. We never found the drive to and back from the office tedious or boring. The 'Boss' used to be our favourite topic of fun and amusement. Jokes, singing songs, witty comments were are companions during travel.

One day while I was driving and we were returning from office, Rajeev got a call on his mobile from some bank call centre. He put it on speaker. "Sir, I am Sameer calling from ABC bank. We want to offer you our credit card. To explain terms and conditions, may I take two minutes of your time, please?"

"Oh! Yes, Sameer bhai, why not? Why two minutes, you can take five minutes as I am sitting in a chauffeur-driven car (as if he is a big boss!) but before that may I take your two minutes of your time, please?"

"Yes Sir! Why not?"

And then to our surprise and amusement, Rajeev started chanting the *Hanuman Chalisa* (verse of Hindu God Hanuman). After he recited the first two lines, the tele-caller understood that Rajeev was making fun of him and so he disconnected the call, never to call again. We laughed at the instant wit of Rajeev who said "Boss, I am fed up with such calls. If I had followed the caller's wish every time, I would have had a dozen credit cards, loans from half a dozen banks and insurance from ten companies. I have hence started this practice."

On reaching home while having dinner, I narrated this funny incident to my sons and thought that they too will be amused but to my dismay, Himanshu said, "Baba, the tele-callers make calls to earn their livelihood. They don't beg or steal. They do their job. They may have a target of calling maybe a hundred people daily without which they cannot go home. I did not like Rajeev uncle making fun of the tele-caller. If you are not interested, you may politely say, "Sorry, I am not interested and disconnect the call. Why insult, humiliate, ridicule or make fun of them?"

It was an eye opener for me. I realised my mistake, never to do it again.

We had a protocol that whosoever's car it is, in case he gets delayed beyond 6:00 pm, the other two would make their own arrangements to return. One such day I had brought my car and my work got over only by 7:30 pm. Instead of travelling alone, I checked if someone from my office and staying in Jeevan Shanti Colony was still in the office. I found Mr Dheeraj Bhanushali who was DM (Legal), still there. He joined me in the car. During our journey, he said, "Sir, some of us from LIC and general insurance companies had formed a co-operative housing society about twenty years ago. We purchased a plot in Kalina (Santacruz East) but the transaction went into litigation. After more than two decades, now the title is transferred in the name of our society. During this period a few members left, a few died. We are hence allowed to induct four new members to our society. If you want to buy a flat in Mumbai, you may be able to buy one in our society's flat scheme."

That sounded pretty good to me and the following Saturday after returning from office I went to the construction site along with Nilambari and Mr Bhanushali. The society had 1BHK and 2BHK flats available for sale at cost of ₹17 lakh and ₹25 lakh respectively. Kalina was a prime location. It was three kilometres from Kurla station to the West and almost the same distance from Santacruz station to the East. The domestic airport was at a distance of just five kilometres. We liked the site but raising money was a problem. I had hardly a lakh or two in my bank account. We came home after telling Mr Bhanushali that we would confirm in the next two days. We discussed it with Aai who said, "I can give you up to ₹4 lakh by raising a loan on my bank FDs. You may return the same to me at your convenience. I contacted Mr S N Bhattacharya, my friend who was the Regional Manager, LIC Housing Finance Limited, Mumbai. He assured me of a loan of ₹12.5 lakh. We were still short of ₹5 lakh to ₹6 lakh to buy a 2BHK flat.

On weekdays, after lunch I used to take a walk along with my friend, Mr S K Roy who was Secretary (Legal). When I told him about buying a flat, he advised me, "Nilesh, if you want to buy a flat in Mumbai, better buy a 2BHK flat. You have two sons. If they get jobs in Mumbai and get married, two families can stay there till they find their own accommodation. Looking at the financial constraint you have, I would advise you to sell off your flat in Pune which will easily fetch you ₹4 lakh to ₹5 lakh."

His advice was invaluable.

On reaching home, we discussed it again. We were still short of ₹3 lakh but since it was not an outright purchase and the payment was to be made on progress of the scheme, we had two years' time to raise the full amount. I paid a token amount and booked a 2BHK flat on the third floor.

The transactions went through as we wanted. In 2004, by the time the flat was ready for possession, I was promoted as Chief (Strategic Business Unit (SBU): P&GS) and was retained in Mumbai. My three other batchmates who got promoted from Mumbai, were all transferred out of Mumbai. God was kind to me.

Along with these good things we also had a traumatic blow within a year. We lost our mother. You cannot expect only good things to happen all the time but her death was sudden.

On promotion, I took charge of the department as Chief (SBU-P&GS) in the Central office. By that time, Mr Atul Shukla with whom I had worked on the GOIB Committee, had become Chairman, LIC. In one of the Central Management Committee (CMC) meetings, he asked us to suggest some innovative ideas to improve the functioning of LIC, which will have a far reaching effect on the growth of the organization.

I always thought that LIC should open its Branches in suburban areas with large population. LIC was not following the basic marketing axiom, 'Be where the customer is'. Out of seventy-three Branches that we had in Mumbai, almost forty were in the Fort and Nariman Point area where offices are located and is not a residential area. We hardly had any presence in the suburbs. I thought of suggesting opening small offices in the suburbs of metros with the 'hub and spoke model'. Due to massive computerization, LIC had stopped recruitment of Assistants (Class 3 employees) hence these offices should be manned with three officers only. It would avoid interference of Unions in day to day working of the Branch and the working would be quite smooth. I thought over it and presented a 'white paper' to the Chairman as a blueprint of Satellite Offices (SOs). A Branch in Fort and Nariman Point area may act as the 'hub' and two to three SOs may function as 'spokes'. Initially, only work relating to new business and premium collection may be done at SO and later some servicing functions may be enabled. He liked the idea and in February 2004 he set up a committee headed by Mr D Krishnan, ED, Mr S K Roy, Chief and me. The Chairman wanted to take it to the Board in March 2004 for consideration as an agenda item. We worked on it relentlessly, worked on costing, what functions can be done there, how much area will be required, how much support should be made available, how these SOs can be linked to the Main Branch through IT linkages etc.

The proposal was put up to the Board which approved opening of a hundred SOs in 2004-05.

During the next year, a hundred SOs were opened in Metro cities. These SOs received such a great response that business in a few SOs even exceeded the business booked at the main Branch of the SO. The SOs have become so popular, that as of now, as against two thousand and forty-three Branches, there are over fifteen hundred SOs. I have great satisfaction of doing something different which proved to be a game-changer.

In the meanwhile, Kaustubh passed his Class XII examination with flying colours securing full marks in Physics, ninety-eight out of hundred in Chemistry and ninety-seven out of hundred in Maths. He got admission in D J Sanghvi College of Engineering, Vile Parle (West) for Electronics Engineering, a Branch of his choice. It was just a kilometre away from our residence. Himanshu, after his graduation, started studying for Civil Services. He joined Chanakya Academy run by a retired IAS officer, Mr Avinash Dharmadhikari for which he stayed in Pune for six months. He appeared for the prelim exams from Mumbai and in the meanwhile, since he had a liking for public speaking, comparing programmes, event management and the like, he got an assignment with a local TV channel, *Aamhi Parlekar*, in which he took interviews of senior citizens. He also arranged few other entertainment programmes for youngsters. During that period, he was dating a girl about which we came to know later when one day he came home with a girl named Prajakta Sarwate who was in final year of M.Sc. in Ruia College, Matunga. She was active in co-curricular activities like singing, theatre, painting, dancing etc. She was seen on the channel as a co-host with Himanshu. What surprised us most was their admission of love in clear terms and saying, "We have decided to marry each other."

It was a shock to us mainly because we thought that his future studies would come to an end and his qualification was not enough to get a good job. Our first impression of Prajakta was good and in our mind we appreciated Himanshu's selection of his life partner but still we were of the view that they should complete their education first and only after getting a good job which will give them a sound financial start should they get married. I said, "Before you decide to get married, I think you should know each other more. Both of you are just past twenty-one. I think that you should complete your education first, become financially independent and then think of getting married."

Both of them nodded their heads. I knew that it was just to respect our feelings but I didn't want to discuss the issue further.

Just eight days thereafter, Himanshu came to me with a glowing face showing me the appointment letter from 'Hutchison Global Services', a call centre in Mumbai, providing services to Vodafone customers in Australia. It mentioned a monthly salary of ₹10,000 per month plus bonus. I laughed and said, "Himanshu, it's good that you have a job now. No work is inferior. Put your heart and soul in whatever you do. Learn the nitty-gritty of business with a dream to start your own call centre one day. I am sorry, but now you have to forget your dream of becoming an IAS officer, but it doesn't matter. If you follow what I told you, you have a bright future ahead of you."

"Baba, I know, I have to join service under compulsion and not by choice. I am not sure if I will own a call centre, but I assure you that I will prove my mettle. It's just the beginning of my life." A twenty-one year old boy, who was otherwise quite carefree and jovial had turned into a responsible man. Soon he started going to work which was not at all easy as the call centre was servicing clients from Australia. A car used to reach home at 3:00 am to pick him up. He used to return home after 1:00 pm. It did disturb his body cycle but not only did he do his job well but earned the Best Employee Award year after year. He made best use of the available time even after his marriage and completed his MBA, earned six Sigma Black belt certification, PMP certification and completed other important courses. He worked in the same company for nine years and got three promotions during the period. Only after the company which was an MNC, was taken over by and Indian company, Tech Mahindra, did he put in his papers to join another MNC, the world's biggest shipping company, Maersk Line as Head (Process Improvement) in Mumbai and later moved to their head office in Copenhagen, Denmark in 2017.

It was decided that after Prajakta completed her M.Sc. and Himanshu was stable in his job, we would get them married in a year or two. But what man proposes, God disposes, came true. We became slaves of circumstances. It so happened that we had to change our plan and get them married within four to five months of their engagement.

Since January 2005 Aai was noticing bleeding from her rectum. Our family physician, Dr Rajan Mehta was treating her but the treatment did not make things better. He referred her to a gynecologist who treated her for piles but the bleeding didn't stop.

Finally, by the end of March 2005 we took her to Dr Sandeep Shah, a gastroenterologist who advised a few pathological tests and a CT scan. He did an ultrasonography and took out some tissues to be sent for biopsy. The biopsy report received after a week, confirmed malignancy. I met Dr Shah who said, "Mr Sathe, I am sorry. But the cancer in her rectum has spread to other parts of her body and it is impossible to operate. Radiation and chemotherapy may add to her agonies rather than cure."

I was shocked. I had a frail hope that the strong lady would fight the cancer with her strong will power as she did in the past. But with the words of Dr Shah, I was dumbstruck. When I reached home, to my surprise, Aai said, "Nilesh, Dr Shah must have confirmed it to be cancer, I know." I was taken aback. The next day, I went to Dr Ajit Phadke in the morning. He saw the reports. He let out a long sigh of despair and said, "Nilesh, it's too late. Nothing is left in our hands. Cancer has spread all over her body. Radiation or chemotherapy would only add to her miseries. Let us avoid it."

I asked him a question, although I knew that the answer to which is known only to God. "Kaka, what is her life span hereafter?"

He said, "Nilesh, I don't know but taking into account her age and the present condition of her health, it would not be more than six months." I told him about Himanshu's marriage. We had a plan to get him married after two to three years. Kaka said, "Nilesh, if you want Tai (my mother) to be present and enjoy the wedding of her first beloved grandson, I suggest that you get him married in the next two to three months."

I came home. By that time, my sister had reached Mumbai. She was very upset on hearing what Ajit Kaka said. In the meanwhile, we met Prajakta's parents who agreed to get them married in the presence of my mother. We finalized 22 May 2005 as their wedding date. The wedding ceremony was held at Kohinoor Hall,

Prabhadevi, in a simple manner with strict no to gifts and bouquets. A large number of relatives, friends and some of my colleagues from LIC were invited.

Aai looked so normal during Himanshu's wedding ceremony that those who were unaware of her disease could never think of it. She attended the wedding with full enthusiasm and looked happy, meeting the guests and relatives who did not have the slightest suspicion that it would be their last meeting with her.

Jeevan Shanti Colony is a unique LIC colony where all classes of employees from officers to sub-staff stay in quarters. There was a community hall which was used for community activities. When the employees would leave for office and the children for schools, wives of Class 4 employees would meet together gossiping and whiling away time over chewing tobacco. Aai started mixing with them. She was a school teacher. She started guiding them towards constructive activities. She would teach them to draw *rangoli*, discuss social issues like the evils of dowry, importance of education, tell them stories from Ramayana and Mahabharata and stories of freedom fighters. She would sometimes hold elocution competitions, drawing competitions, *rangoli* competitions and give them prizes from her own money. Although I was a high ranking officer in LIC, many ladies and children from the colony recognized me as the son of Sathe Aaji (which means grandma). I am proud of that.

During her terminal illness Aai used to become unconscious; she would hallucinate to have gone to the community hall and was speaking with the wives of Class 4 employees. Such was her passion. I was told that when pain becomes unbearable, one becomes unconscious so that one doesn't feel the pain. Once the pain subsided and she became conscious, she started reciting *Bhagavad-Gita*, *Ramaraksha* and other *Sanskrit shlokas.* She never cried even when she suffered acute pain during those days.

I had to go to Jaipur on 17 December 2005 for a P&GS conference and review meeting of North Zone units. My sister, Nilima Tai, had come to Mumbai then. She used to visit for a week every month to take care of Aai. I asked Tai if I should go to Jaipur. She said, "Don't worry. I am here with Aai, you go." Still, before leaving for the airport, I asked Aai, "Should I go?" She said, "Duty first." I left, never thinking that those will be her last words. I reached Jaipur, went to 'The Park' hotel, where the conference and stay for all officers was arranged. All the officers had reached already. I met them for dinner. While I was about to start dinner, I got a call from Nilambari sharing with me the shattering news, "Aai is no more."

I informed the Chairman and other senior officers that I would be returning to Mumbai by the next available flight. I cancelled my ticket, booked a fresh ticket for the next day's 6:30 am flight from Jaipur to Mumbai, skipped dinner, asked the Regional Manager to advise all the officials to assemble in the conference hall for a quick review session at 10:00 pm post dinner.

Only at 11:30 -12:00 at night, when the review of all the units was over, I informed them of the death of my mother and told them that the conference would be chaired by the RM (P&GS) in my absence. I also told them the last two words uttered by my mother, "Duty first". Their grief was overwhelming.

I returned to my room. I called up Nilambari again. She informed me that Aai's body was kept in the room with air-conditioning on. She had informed most of our relatives and acquaintances. It was impossible for me to get sleep that night. I kept on recalling memories of my mother. Finally, I got ready at 5:00 am and left the hotel to catch the flight to Mumbai.

When I saw her, a period of over twelve hours had passed after her death, but she looked as calm as she always looked. She had a peaceful death. My maternal uncle, Bandu mama, who was more like her son, draped her in a new saree brought by him as per the tradition. In the presence of relatives, friends and colleagues, the last rites were performed in the Santacruz-Vile Parle crematorium. Tai and Sudhir stayed for fifteen days thereafter to comfort us. One day I asked Tai, "Aai loved me so much, then why did she die when I was not around?" Tai enfolded me in her arms and stroked my head. Wiping my tears she said, "Nilesh, it is often seen that when the death of the most beloved comes near, God separates the two affectionate ones, to help the one alive bear the loss. As you are highly emotional, Aai ensured that you are away at the time of her death." I agreed with her logic. As our friends and acquaintances from Nagpur could not attend the funeral, we decided to have the first death anniversary rituals done in our Nagpur house, where Aai stayed for most part of her life.

Living in Jeevan Shanti Colony without her was becoming difficult for us. As it is, quarters in Prabhadevi for my rank were available. We decided to shift to Prabhadevi. Meanwhile, the Kalina flat was also ready for occupancy. Against their wish, we shifted Himanshu and Prajakta to the flat in Kalina and we shifted to a spacious 2BHK flat on the seventh floor of Antariksha building, Prabhadevi, overlooking Siddhi Vinayak Temple.

Kaustubh completed his Bachelor's Degree in Engineering in 2005. He wanted to obtain a Master of Science degree from the US. He got admission in Stony Brook University, New York and left. As against six members in the Santacruz quarters, when we shifted to Antariksha, we were down to two. We stayed in Jeevan Shanti Colony for almost ten years. Aai always had a soft corner for children of poor families. She always used to say, "The poor students do not get facilities of coaching classes, costly guides etc. which the children of rich parents benefit from." Keeping that in mind, we created an endowment of ₹10,000 in her memory with the Jeevan Shanti Residents' Association with a request to pay its interest to the topper student in SSC who stayed in Class IV quarters. Jeevan Shanti Colony may forget me but not Aai, with the endowment fund in her name that benefits poor students.

Lessons Learnt...

- Don't insult, humiliate or ridicule anybody for doing his job, if you are not interested in buying, politely decline.
- Always follow the basic marketing axiom, 'Be where the customer is'.
- Be compassionate to the poor.
- Duty first.

VIII

Five Golden Years in 'Antariksha'

Our stay in Antariksha was a memorable one with respect to my personal and professional growth. We were blessed with a grandson, I was promoted on time, I was given an assignment to start a new marketing channel in LIC, I was made in charge of the prestigious North Zone Delhi. All of it happened in a span of just five years.

LIC owned ten flats in the twenty-three storey building, Antariksha. I was allotted a flat on the seventh floor, overlooking Siddhi Vinayak Temple. It was a West facing flat with cross ventilation to the East. On a clear day, the Bandra-Worli Sea-link was also visible. Since there was not a single high-rise structure right up to the sea, the cool breeze in the evening was enviable.

By then I had completed three years as Chief (SBU-P&GS). The progress of the Strategic Business Unit was well appreciated by the top management. Designing gratuity, leave encashment, pension and group insurance schemes for public and private sector companies including banks and financial Institutions along with managing funds set aside by the companies for the same was the function of SBU-P&GS. I was regularly meeting the Corporate Heads and CFOs to convince them of the need for setting aside funds for their statutory and non-statutory liabilities towards employees. I was able to garner funds in thousands of crores from big corporate houses like SAIL, NCL, Bank of India, Bank of Baroda, Canara Bank, Bank of Maharashtra, Mahindra & Mahindra, HUL,

ONGC, Indian Oil, HPCL, Reliance Industries Ltd and many other leading business houses. I used to plan my tour to five important cities every month to meet the corporate officials. During my four years tenure in SBU, I visited almost all state capitals, big cities and industrial towns in India. Meeting CEOs/CFOs for getting new business and if they were our existing clients, meeting them to get their feedback on LIC servicing used to be the purpose of the tours. I used to share with them the strengths of LIC and the changes LIC was bringing for 'customer's delight'.

LIC gave me the position which enabled me to meet highly respected CEOs like Mr Nandan Nilekani of Infosys, Mr M B N Rao, CMD of Canara Bank, Mr Bhaskar Bhat, MD of Titan, Mr P K Bishnoi, Finance Director of Vizag Steel, Mr S R Kulkarni, trustee of JNPT and many more. I learnt a lot from them, mainly their simplicity, courteous behaviour and mannerism. When I met Mr Nandan Nilekani, I never imagined that he would be wearing jeans and a T-shirt in office. I had gone to hand over the Group Gratuity Policy for Infosys employees. I found him a simple and down to earth person. Even if he was from an Engineering/IT background, he asked me many questions related to finance and investments. I learnt that when you are meeting such top-class industry leaders, you should always be well-prepared.

Communication is the key in marketing. In marketing it is taught, 'Never argue with the customer. You may win the argument but lose the customer'. The second teaching is, use the term 'Yes, but...' while pushing your argument, and that is what I followed while dealing with Mumbai Port Trust (MbPT).

MbPT employees had a pension scheme. Since the port is over one hundred and twenty-five years old, a good number of retired but living employees were paid pension every month through Money Order (MO). The Trust had two representatives of workers as Trustees viz. Mr S R Kulkarni and Dr Shanti Patel. They used to frequently receive complaints of late receipt of MO, money delivered to the wrong person etc. MOs for pension were being sent in the names of many such retired workers who had died long ago. The Trustees decided to hand over the job of pension payment to LIC and had hence called us for a discussion. We met at their office at Ballard Pier, Mumbai. A few senior officers from LIC accompanied me. We listened to their problem. It was suggested by them that the job of settlement of monthly pension to over ten thousand retired employees be managed by LIC, for which they were ready to pay us the service charge. We were legally not allowed to undertake such activity even for fees. But I didn't say 'No' outright. I took a week's time to study the proposal and assured them to come back soon. We discussed it in our office. I found a business proposition and revenue generation stream in the proposal but the question was that legally we could not do this job. How could we fit ourselves to their requirement while remaining within our legal frame-work, was the questions. LIC had a mandate to pay pension if the corpus is handed over to LIC. If it was possible to get the corpus, it would not only help LIC get huge funds for investment but would also open the floodgates for business with other ports as well.

I went there after a week and made a presentation to the Trustees on how we could take up the job of pension settlement free of charge provided the corpus of funds towards the annuitants (pensioners) was given to us. I told them that it might be done in phases and once we have fifty per cent corpus with us, we would start the pension payment with direct credit to the bank account of the annuitants. I knew that the views of the employees' representatives of the Trust, Mr S R Kulkarni and Dr Shanti Patel would be vital. Hence, after the meeting, I met them separately. They were keen on giving the funds to LIC where the money was secured, being a corporation formed by the Government of India. They were convinced of our capability to pay pension on time and our competence in managing their funds. The workers had full faith in their two leaders who had always protected their interests. I learnt that our proposal was whole-heartedly supported by the two Trustees in the Trustee meeting and it was decided that the corpus would be handed over to LIC for management and when it crosses ₹6,000 crore, LIC would start paying pension to the retired workers. An initial cheque of ₹1,000 crore was handed over to me in a month's time. MbPT started collecting bank account details of the retired workers and within eight months, when the corpus crossed ₹6,000 crore, LIC started paying pension in a seamless manner. Once this proposal got through, we got funds from other Ports like Kandla Port, Chennai Port, Vizag Port and all the other ports in India thereafter. As of now, LIC is managing Pension Funds of over ₹25,000 crore of various ports in India.

Later when I met Mr S R Kulkarni, he complimented me and his words are a treasure for me. He said, "Mr Sathe, in the first meeting itself you could have declined the proposal as it was not fitting into the legal framework of LIC. I appreciate your perseverance and, in the process, you got substantial premium for LIC." Dr Shanti Patel who was also present there said, "Our issue was different. We knew that some employees were pocketing pensions of employees who had died. The office staff used to take a huge amount of overtime every month for filling up MO forms. We wanted this to stop but they were also our members hence we thought that the best way to streamline payouts was to involve LIC, which being a Government organization, no eyebrows may be raised. Thanks for streamlining pension payouts."

In a competitive set up, it's not easy to get new clients and to keep the existing ones in your hold is also a big challenge. Sometimes, one has to use 'unreal threats' as a tactic in order to make clients realize that they will incur huge losses if they decide to move their business to another insurance company. I once had to use this tactic to retain our Group Gratuity client, M/S DCM Shriram from Delhi.

During the pre-independence era, two brothers, Shriram and Bharat set up a cloth mill in Delhi and named it as Delhi Cloth Mill (DCM), which prospered in the sixties and seventies. It listed its shares on the Stock Exchange. LIC was holding about eight per cent shares of the company, even though the company had not declared dividend of a single rupee for the past many years. There was no need for me to go through the history and the financials of the company, as I was not posted in the Investment Department of LIC. However, it became necessary because we received a notice from the company of withdrawing their Gratuity and Pension Funds managed by us. We were managing their funds of about

₹22 crore which was considerably less compared to the total fund of thousands of crores managed by us. But Mr L S Rawat, Manager of our P&GS unit of Delhi, informed me that DCM intended to handover funds to an insurance company started by a bank and the bank had promised them a substantial loan if they did so. I thought of meeting top officials of the company. On the appointed date and time, I reached their office along with Mr Rawat. Before going for the meeting, I had met Mr Sushobhan Sarker, ED (Investment) and had told him that I may be required to give the company an 'unreal threat' and explained what I might say to which he agreed.

During our meeting, the Chairman of DCM was there along with his team of five officers. I said, "I received your notice intimating your intention to withdraw funds from LIC. Are there any servicing issues? Are you not happy with the return you are getting from LIC on your funds?"

The Chairman said, "No, Mr Sathe, that's not the case. We have banking operations with a particular bank and they are pressuring us to give our employees' Gratuity and Superannuation Fund to the insurance company promoted by them. Our Board has, hence passed a resolution to withdraw funds from LIC and shift the same to a particular insurance company." He handed over a copy of the Board resolution and said, "Since the Board has decided, I can't help."

I replied, "It's alright. ₹22 crore is not a big amount for LIC which is managing a fund of over ₹4 lakh crore. I can just draw a cheque and pay it to you. But it appears that you have forgotten that LIC also holds substantial equity stake in your company. It's about eight per cent. In spite of the fact that your company didn't pay dividend of a single rupee during the last eight years, LIC has not offloaded its investment in your company. Do you know why? It's because we have respect for Sir Shriram, a public-spirited philanthropist and one of the trend-setting visionary leaders of the business community during the British era which became India's largest business group. We have respect for the indigenous entrepreneurs. But you don't seem to have similar respect for the Government owned and the largest Indian life insurance company in India. Just imagine, if we offload our equity holding in your company in the share market, what will be its impact on your market capitalization. It will come crashing down. Paying ₹22 crore is not difficult for LIC but the decision to withdraw may prove detrimental for your company. You may take two more days to reconsider your decision. If you still wish to surrender the scheme just inform us. Your application will be processed and you will get your funds. I am leaving now. Thanks for the time given. God bless!"

I was observing how the brightness on the face of the Chairman was fading with my every word. He requested me to discuss the issue for some more time but I pretended that I might miss the flight and left.

The next day when I reached office, my P.A. told me that Chairman, DCM Shriram, wanted to talk to me. I asked her to connect the call. He said, "Sir, we are reconsidering our decision of withdrawal of funds from LIC."

Actually speaking, LIC might not have reduced its equity stake in the company just because the company withdrew its gratuity fund management from LIC. But if LIC had sold the shares of the company, the share price and the market capitalization of the company would have certainly come crashing down.

In my address to the P&GS marketing officials, I used to tell this instance followed by a story of Gautam Buddha.

Once to a dreaded poisonous snake, Buddha ordered not to bite any human being. Knowing well that the snake wouldn't bite due to Buddha's orders, even children started hitting it with sticks and stones. After a few days when Buddha was passing from there, he found the snake almost dead. He understood what might have happened and said, "Oh dear snake, I had asked you not to bite but it appears that you gave up hissing too. If you hiss, nobody would dare trouble you."

The threat given by me was like 'hissing'. Sometimes 'hissing' is required to retain an existing customer.

One day, the Chairman, Mr Vijayan called me and said, "Mr Sathe, every year LIC issues over fifty lakh premium receipts from its two thousand Branches and a few hundred SOs. It always worries me that if the customers have to wait for a long time to pay their premium in Branches, sooner or later, it will impact our business. The queues at the cash counter should come down. I want you to think over it and submit a blueprint within a week."

Increasing the number of cash counters was an easy option. But it was impractical as LIC had stopped recruitment of clerical cadre for over the last fifteen years. LIC used to appoint 'Assistant' and not 'Clerk cum Cashier' as was done by banks. That being so, the Assistants were always reluctant to work as cashiers. A way out was to amend staff regulations but it would have taken time and it involved approval of the Finance Ministry. So, the only solution to the problem that came to my mind was 'outsourcing'. I prepared a blueprint which had three suggestions:

- Tie up with Banks and provide an interface to them so that they can issue receipts like LIC Branches. The Bank Branches may be authorized to issue premium receipts for a nominal fee.
- Using Common Service Centres (CSC). Some states like MP, AP had started such CSCs and had authorized them to collect property tax, water bills, electricity bills etc. Making the interface available to CSCs and paying them some fees per collection.
- Authorizing club member Agents of LIC to collect premium by making the interface available to them.

Of course, the Chairman wanted a detailed foolproof system. Accordingly, I submitted a detailed paper mentioning how it can be done and how it cannot be misused. If the collecting Agent doesn't deposit the amount collected by the next working day in LIC's office, automatically his premium collection facility should stop. Daily limit of collection should be prescribed in such a way that even if he defaults, the amount should be easily recoverable out of the commission due etc.

Mr Vijayan liked the proposal. He called Mr Debashish Tarafdar, ED (IT) and asked him to find from Axis Bank, which was our Bancassurance partner, if it would like to connect to the LIC's IT-system to issue renewal premium receipts like a regular Branch of LIC and if so, get it done as quickly as possible.

In a month thereafter, it was tested if an Axis Bank Branch was able to issue premium receipts to a customer. It was also checked that if the bank Branch does not deposit the collection on the next working day, the facility of collection would stop. It was also tested that the facility restarted once the collection was deposited. After the trial run was successful, Mr Tarafdar confirmed it to Mr Vijayan. By that time, the Legal Department had finalized the draft of authorization and after entering into an agreement with Axis Bank, the first receipt was issued by Axis Bank to the customer. The same facility was later extended to MP on-line, AP on-line, CSCs and to hundred Top Agents of LIC.

I was happy that my suggestion saw the light of the day. However, the number of receipts issued by these premium collection centres was negligible even after a period of two years of its implementation. The monitoring of alternate premium collection centres was done by the Marketing Department. I had, by then, become ED and was heading a new Marketing Channel.

In one of the Central Management Committee (CMC) meetings, Mr Vijayan expressed his displeasure over efforts of the Marketing Department in promoting the scheme. He asked if some other department was ready to take the responsibility of pushing the initiative aggressively. I raised my hand. Since the scheme was conceived by me two years before and had not caught momentum, I was eager to find the reasons for the lukewarm response and to take corrective action.

Chairman said, "I am happy that you have volunteered. I want you to ensure that two months from now, the number of receipts issued by these alternate channels should increase ten folds."

"Sir I won't commit right away but will quickly study the reasons and formulate the action plan as to how the number of receipts will go up soon."

"That's the spirit." Chairman complimented me.

I had mastered the 'Problem Solving Technique' during my posting in the HR Department in Kolkata. Identify the problem, define it, find alternatives, make a choice and implement it. Evaluate results and if necessary, start the process again. I went to the office of our Agent, Mr Anand Jathan to understand the process of issuing receipts. For that, I had carried a cheque with me for my policy premium which was due. The Assistant in his office logged in with his password. It took three to four minutes to connect to the LIC server and by the time, the receipt was issued to me, ten to twelve minutes had passed. Mr Jathan said, "Sir, if it takes ten minutes to issue one receipt, who will be enthused in doing this work? Also, the receipt gets printed on the first page while the space for authorized signature is on the second page. If someone removes the first page of the receipt issued by me and replaces it with a different first page, will I not get into trouble? Should the receipt not be on as single page and look like the regular receipt issued by LIC? We have to spend on the salary of an Assistant issuing receipts, spend on paper, internet, computer, printer and LIC pays us only ₹3 per receipt against ₹10 it pays to Axis Bank." I understood the problem. I took up all the IT related queries with my friend, Mr B Venugopal, ED (IT) who later became MD of LIC. He was quick in understanding the problems and solved them within a fortnight. In the meanwhile, I submitted a note for approval to the Chairman giving justification for increasing expense-reimbursement to Agents from ₹3 to ₹7 per receipt. I knew that he wouldn't agree for the same but as is said in marketing, "If you want a pistol, ask the boss for a cannon." He approved an increase to ₹5 per receipt which is what I wanted. The same was later increased to ₹10.

The time taken by the marketing department to issue a letter of authorization and password to the Agent was taking months. Moreover, there was no one to guide the agent in case he had some problem. I requested Mr Venugopal to prepare on a CD, for the guidance of Agents with step-wise guide right from turning on the computer upto the issuance of a receipt. He quickly did it. I started sending a demo-CD to every Agent along with his letter of authorization and password. We supplied back-lit sign boards saying 'Authorized Premium Collection Centre - Premium Point' with the Agent's name and asked them to display those outside their offices. With my heart set on popularizing an alternate channel for premium collection, results were bound to come. In a year, the number of receipts issued per day increased, not just ten folds but over hundred folds. As of now, over fifty per cent of premium receipts are issued outside LIC Branches mainly through three thousand two hundred premium points of LIC Agents.

The Chairman, Mr Vijayan's dream and desire that customers shouldn't be made to wait at LIC's cash counters for premium payment, has now come true. I have great satisfaction of being a part of the team which implemented the project.

During my time as Chief (SBU-P&GS), the Government of India wanted LIC to design and implement a Social Security Scheme for the welfare of the heads of families that were Below Poverty Line (BPL). I had the honour of making a presentation to the Prime Minister of India, Dr Manmohan Singh, for this particular group scheme. My department discussed and formulated a scheme wherein the insured beneficiaries between eighteen and sixty years of age would be covered for ₹30,000 for natural death, ₹75,000 for accidental death and ₹37,500 for permanent partial disability like loss of one limb, eye etc. due to an accident. It had an added benefit of scholarship at ₹1,200 per annum to be given to the beneficiary's two children at a maximum, studying from Class IX to Class XII. The premium worked out to be ₹200 per beneficiary out of which ₹100 was to be subsidized through Social Security Fund managed by LIC. The balance of ₹100 could be paid by the State Government or an NGO or a corporate through its social funding.

After the Chairman's approval, it was sent to the Ministry of Finance (MoF). I went to Delhi in November 2006 to discuss the scheme with the officials of the MoF. But till the first week of February 2007 there was no response from the Ministry. Suddenly on 10 February 2007 the Chairman received a call from the Joint Secretary, MoF asking to suggest a suitable name for the scheme. He called me. I was happy to know that the scheme was likely to see the light of the day. "The name should be easy to understand and universally accepted across all states," he said. We thought of Bhagyalaxmi, Bhagyodaya, Beema Shakti etc. but I knew that the Government was concerned about the common man (aam admi) and hence we proposed the name 'Aam Admi Bima Yojana (AABY)'. Mr Vijayan liked it and the same was conveyed to the MoF. Soon thereafter, Mr Vijayan got a letter from MoF according to which LIC was invited to make a 15-minute presentation at 9:00 am on 22 February 2007 to the Prime Minister of India in the presence of Mr Montek Singh Ahluwalia, Deputy Chairman, Planning Commission, and other officials of MoF.

Mr Vijayan called me, showed me the letter and said, "As the scheme is conceived by you, I want you to go to Delhi on 22 February 2007 to make a presentation to the Prime Minister." I was surprised. Generally, the Chairman himself would have seized such an opportunity, but by asking me to go, I was happy that he found me worthy of it. I was not even an ED then.

I prepared fifteen slides, rehearsed to confirm that the time to explain the scheme was not exceeding fifteen minutes, got it approved by the Chairman and sent it to MoF the next day. I got approval for the presentation and as decided, I reached Committee Room No. 2 in South Block at 8:45 am along with our Regional Manager (P&GS), Delhi. I was told that the PM was attending the meeting along with Deputy Chairman, Planning Commission, Mr Montek Singh Ahluwalia and the Cabinet Secretary, Mr B K Chaturvedi. They entered the committee room right at 9:00 am. I stood up, introduced myself and said, "As directed by the Government, we have designed a Social Security Scheme for the poor, for your kind consideration." I started my Power Point presentation, at the end of which I invited questions.

Mr Montek Singh asked, "Is LIC capable of implementing the scheme on an all India basis or do we start a pilot with a few states first?" I was ready with a reply. "Sir, I am confident that LIC would be able to implement it on an all India basis through its sixty-nine P&GS offices spread in all the states."

"How many beneficiaries will be covered in the first year?"

"Sir, at least one crore."

The three of them discussed something in a low tone. Finally, the Cabinet Secretary asked me, "Mr Sathe, are you sure that the scheme is doable on such a large scale?"

"Sir, I am confident that LIC can do it."

He said, "Okay" and they left.

Secretary, MoF complimented me and said, "Good presentation." I thanked him and we left. On reaching the LIC guest house, I narrated every detail to Mr Vijayan on phone. On hearing me, he said, "Mr Sathe, I think that the Aam Admi Bima Yojana will be announced by the Finance Minister in his Budget speech." His words came true. We were eagerly awaiting the Union Budget presented by Mr P Chidambaram of 28 February 2007. While announcing the scheme, he said, "Out of the premium of ₹200 per person per annum, the Central Government would pay ₹100 out of its Social Security Fund and I appeal to the State Governments to contribute the balance. I expect that seventy lakh beneficiaries will be covered in the first year."

Soon we finalized the design of pamphlets, leaflets in major Indian languages, sent letters to Chief Secretaries of all the State Governments under the signature of the Chairman, LIC, asked the P&GS officials in State headquarters to seek appointment and meet the concerned bureaucrats and convince them about the efficacy of the scheme. In the meanwhile, Mr Chidambaram wrote to all the Chief Ministers advising them to implement the scheme.

In spite of all these efforts, no State Government came forward to implement the Scheme till the end of June 2007. Our officials started losing hearts but I kept on telling them not to lose patience. Finally, Government of Rajasthan replied to the letter sent by LIC and wanted a Senior Official of LIC to discuss the nitty-gritty of the scheme. I went to Jaipur to meet Mrs Vasundhara Raje Scindia, the Chief Minister. She was impressed with the element of scholarship ingrained into the scheme. She instructed the Chief Secretary to give me the list of beneficiaries in a soft copy, upon my insistence. She told the Chief Secretary that Rajasthan should be the first state to implement Aam Admi Bima Yojana. It was just within a month thereafter, that I was invited to receive a cheque for ₹15 crore for covering fifteen lakh poor beneficiaries. I handed over the policy document in exchange for the cheque. The event was widely covered by the media and newspapers.

Mr R R alias Abasaheb Patil was the Deputy Chief Minister of Maharashtra. He called me for discussion. I told him, "Although Rajasthan is a non-Congress ruled state, it became the first state to implement the scheme and it has benefitted fifteen lakh poor households. I wish that Maharashtra becomes the first Congress-ruled state to implement the scheme." He took details of the scheme and asked his personal secretary to submit the required information to me. Incidentally, his personal secretary was Mr Nitin Gadre, IAS, whom I knew since his childhood. He ensured that a list of five lakh beneficiaries would be submitted to me soon and Maharashtra became the second state to implement the scheme. I was handed over a cheque for ₹5 crore towards the State Government's share of premium. It received wide coverage in the national media which helped us encourage other states to join the scheme and by December 2007 itself, LIC had covered seventy lakh beneficiaries as wished by the Finance Minister in his Union Budget speech. We issued a press release. A leading Marathi newspaper from Mumbai, Nav Shakti, published my interview taken by renowned writer and columnist, Mr Vinayak Kulkarni. During the interview, he asked me, "How many lives do you think will be covered by March 2008?" I said, "one crore." I was happy that actually we covered more than one Crore and five lakh beneficiaries by the end of March 2008. AABY continued for over ten years and LIC implemented it extremely well over years. I was also interviewed on various TV channels. Nav-Shakti announced an award for me which was given at a function in Dinanath Natyagruha, Vile Parle, at the hands of Dr Snehalata Deshmukh, Vice Chancellor, Mumbai University. While receiving the award, I remembered my mother and wished that she was alive to see the honour bestowed upon me.

In 2008, my promotion to the cadre of Executive Director (ED) was due. Kaustubh completed his Master of Science degree and joined Cummins in the US. Graduation (convocation) is a great event there and is celebrated as a ceremony. He wanted us to be present for the graduation ceremony which was due in May 2008. As my promotion was due (about which I was confident) and it was necessary for me to take charge immediately on being promoted, we decided that only Nilambari would attend the graduation ceremony. After attending the graduation ceremony, she visited Niagara Falls, stalactite mines near Washington D.C., the Statue of Liberty among other places. She visited our relatives in New York and Washington and returned after three weeks.

The year 2007-08 was a memorable one in my life. In July 2007 after the Rajasthan Government introduced AABY for the state, I went to Chairman, Mr Vijayan, to show him photographs of the function. He seemed to be at leisure. He called for a cup of tea and said, "Mr Sathe, Agents are the backbone of LIC. You know that in the past we used to elevate them to the level of Development Officer (DO) with twenty five per cent vacancies reserved for Agents. But due to Court's intervention, during the last five to six years, Agents don't have a separate quota and have to compete with open market candidates, as a result of which hardly any Agent is able to become a DO. We need to do something to elevate them to a higher level, equivalent to DO but not as employees. I want you to think about it and submit to me a white paper on how it can be done." I assured him of such a paper within a week.

I asked a few senior club member Agents known to me if they would be able to appoint Agents and supervise them, if given a chance and what remuneration they expected. Most of them were thrilled with the idea and said that they were ready to do so at whatever remuneration LIC might give. My discussion with them confirmed my hypothesis that if the senior Agents are given an opportunity to work as DOs, but not on the rolls of LIC, they will be able to do good business.

I prepared a working paper on 'How to utilize LIC's Club Member Agents in increasing insurance business by allowing them to identify, train, mentor new Agents and get business done from them'. Mr Vijayan liked the idea. In order to make a proper framework of the scheme, he formed a Committee under

Chairmanship of Mr A K Sahoo, ED (Marketing). I was one of the other three members of the committee. We studied the Insurance Act, 1938, IRDA rules, regulations and guidelines. We ensured the following:

- Multi-level Marketing (MLM) was prohibited, so we ensured that the scheme didn't have the same.
- The remuneration payable to the Senior Agent should always be less than the one paid to DOs.
- The Senior Agent shouldn't ignore his own business.
- He should not appoint only his own close relatives as agents and divert business to them.
- There should not be any fixed cost to LIC. He should get rewarded, if he does business and should get nothing if he fails to do any new business.

Finally, we submitted our report to the Chairman. We knew that the DOs and their association would oppose the scheme vehemently and hence all discussions were kept highly confidential.

Mr Vijayan got the scheme approved by the Board in March 2008 but I came to know about it only a few days before my promotion in April 2008 when Mr Vijayan, after P&GS final business figures were consolidated on 8April 2008 called me and said, "Mr Sathe, I know P&GS has done well. Congratulations. I am giving you urgent and important work." He gave me a copy of the Board Note on the 'Chief Life Insurance Advisors' (CLIA) Scheme'. He told me that the note was approved by the Board verbatim and wanted me to take it forward. He called Ms Navin Kaul, Chief (Legal), and instructed us to first consult the solicitors to tell us if the scheme was perfect from legal point of view.

We met Advocate Snehal Paranjape and requested her to advise if the scheme, as approved by the Board could be taken forward without any legal hassles. She said, "Unless you give me a full, properly drafted scheme, I won't be able to advise you. Moreover, if you are afraid that the scheme may be challenged by the DO Association in the High Court, we may have to file a Caveat in all the twenty-four High Courts. This can be done only when the scheme is announced and uploaded on your website."

Obviously, without drafting the scheme per-se containing eligibility, age, functions, benefits, penalties etc., and getting it approved by the Chairman, there was no going ahead.

In the meanwhile, promotions were announced and I was promoted as ED (Marketing/CLIA). Not many knew the full form of 'CLIA' which was Chief Life Insurance Advisors. I too kept it under my sleeve. I had completed eleven years of my service in Mumbai. While two of my batchmates promoted from Mumbai were sent out, I was lucky to continue in Mumbai on promotion. Posting to a newly created department meant my continuation for at least three more years in Mumbai.

I met the Chairman, thanked him for my promotion and retention in Mumbai. I informed him about our discussions with Advocate Paranjape and expressed the urgency to draft the scheme. I wanted him to advise me in the matter. He said, "Mr Sathe, many of our high performing Agents are not highly qualified. You should design a scheme for them which is easy to understand. There should not be an element of fixed cost. I don't want LIC to pay them if they don't perform. It should be cost efficient for LIC, meaning that for the same amount of new business premium brought by a CLIA and a DO, the CLIA should be paid at least twenty per cent less than the DO. You are good at Maths. Design a scheme and submit it to me for approval as soon as possible."

Based on his suggestions, I designed a scheme which was easy to understand. The payout calculations were easy. A CLIA was supposed to identify, train, mentor Agents and on their passing test of IRDA, they were supposed to do LIC business. In order to ensure that a CLIA doesn't ignore his own LIC business, it was proposed that if a CLIA lost his Club Membership, he would lose his 'CLIAship' too. He was not allowed to supervise more than twenty-five Agents and was entitled to benefits only after he had five Agents on roll. The benefit payable to the CLIA was based on the commission earned by the supervised Agents. It was easy to understand and calculate how much a CLIA would earn.

After discussion with Mr Vijayan, some changes were made and the scheme was finally approved by him. I gave a copy of the scheme to the Advocate for perusal and advice. On the next day she advised us to go ahead. We decided to post the scheme on our website on Thursday and file 'caveats' in all the twenty-four High Courts on Friday morning, as soon as the Courts opened, since Courts are closed on Saturday and Sunday. Advocate Paranjape gave us the draft of the caveat. Ms Navin Kaul coordinated with the Managers (Legal) of all the twenty-four divisions where High Courts were located and ensured that the caveats were filed. She confirmed to me by 12 noon that the caveats were filed in all the twenty-four High Courts. I was at least partially relieved. The caveat ensured that even if someone filed a case against implementation of the scheme, no court would pass a stay without hearing us. Half the battle was won as later I came to know that a DO association was to file a case in a High Court with a request to 'stay' the implementation of the scheme but when they came to know that a caveat had already been filed, the DO association didn't proceed further.

RMs (CLIA) were posted in each Zone and one Manager (CLIA) was posted in each Division. The Scheme was sent on email to all the 15,000 Club Member Agents having CM/ZM/DM Club Membership and who were below sixty years of age. We got a stupendous response from these Agents and by the end of first year itself, the new CLIA channel's share in the new business of LIC was over three per cent which was even higher than the business done by the 'Bancassurance' channel set up a couple of years before.

The first year was quite hectic for me. Getting the IT system in place for the payment of benefits to CLIAs, training the Managers, the CLIAs and their Supervised Agents to ensure that these Agents pass the IRDA test. Some CLIAs failed to appoint the minimum required five Agents, they were given an extension of one more year.

I continued as ED (CLIA) for three years. By the end of the third year, the number of Agents supervised by CLIAs crossed sixty-two thousand. The scheme was a grand success. As of now, over twelve per cent of LIC's new business premium is contributed by CLIAs.

The scheme had another advantage. The DOs started taking care of their Agents. The scheme paved the way for the Club Member Agents' elevation. As of now, in many Branches, the business done by a CLIA is more than the business done by the top performing DO. It started a new era of healthy competition among marketing forces.

During these years on the family front as well, there was good progress. Kaustubh returned from the US after working there for a year and joined the Aeronautics Dept in IIT Powai, Mumbai, as Research Associate. After gaining experience for a year, he joined Bosch in Coimbatore. Himanshu and Prajakta were blessed with a son who was named Kanha. The icing on the cake was my promotion and retention in Mumbai. But the best was yet to come. After my three years stint as ED in Mumbai, I was posted as Additional Zonal Manager, North Zone, Delhi. The then existing Zonal Manager, Mr V K Sinha was to retire in June 2011 after which I was to be made Zonal Manager.

ZM Delhi is always regarded as a coveted post as it's a big zone comprising of seven states from J&K to Rajasthan and one union territory of Chandigarh. Since the Ministry of Finance (MoF), now called the Department of Financial Services (DFS) was located in our building, a lot of liaisoning was required with the Government officials. My posting came as a surprise to many. There were many aspirants who were senior to me eyeing the post of ZM Delhi but probably Mr Vijayan considered me for the post as a reward for the good work done by me in establishing a new marketing channel.

Lessons Learnt...

- Communication is the key in marketing. Never argue with a customer, you may win the argument but lose the customer.
- Use the term, 'Yes, but...' while pushing your argument.
- In a competitive set up it's not easy to keep the existing clients in your hold. It's a big challenge. You may have to use unconventional methods to keep them in your hold.

IX

Delhi: Dreadful Days

I took charge as Additional Zonal Manager at Delhi on 1 May 2011, the foundation day of Maharashtra state and my birthday as well. We occupied the ZM's bungalow at Sundar Nagar. By then Nilambari had completed twenty-eight years of service as Assistant in LIC. She decided to resign from her services as she said, "I don't want to work under you when you have become the Zonal Manager." Although she had a good work record, she never applied for a promotion because in that case, she thought, she would not be able to do justice to her office work and household responsibilities. Her decision to put in her papers made me happy since I thought that she may get some leisure time after a hectic twenty-eight years of managing both, home and office. During the fourteen long years of posting in Mumbai many good things happened in my life like four on-time promotions, streamlined education from SSC to graduation of my sons, Himanshu's wedding, becoming grandparents etc. but my mother's death was an irreparable loss to our family. She would have felt so happy to stay in a spacious bungalow in Delhi but it was not to happen. It was a two-storey bungalow with eight rooms a lawn and a courtyard. Kaustubh had left his job in Bosch Coimbatore and was working at Maruti Suzuki, Gurugram (formerly Gurgaon). He had taken a house on rent in Gurugram. As soon as we settled in our bungalow, Kaustubh vacated his house and shifted to stay with us. He started going to the factory by car.

There were 17 Divisions in the North Zone. I was supposed to tour these Divisions for Marketing Conferences. I started my tour to the divisions from Amritsar. I chose Amritsar because I wanted to take blessings of Waheguru, Guru Gobind Singh and visit the Golden Temple. Gurudwara Prabandhak Samiti (managing committee of Gurudwara, the temple) honoured me with a sword and two photo frames of the Golden Temple. I also visited Jallianwala Bagh where innocent Indians were shot dead by the British.

On my return to Delhi, I visited my college friend Nitin Gadkari who was then the National President of the Bharatiya Janata Party (BJP). I gave him the sword and said, "It's more useful to you for protecting the weak and destroying the evils in society." It was a symbolic gift that I gave him. He accepted it wholeheartedly.

I always thought of making a short film which would promote youngsters to become LIC Agents. There was a general feeling that only if a young graduate doesn't get a job for three to four years after graduation, he takes up LIC agency to try his luck. I wanted to show that an LIC agency was a good avenue of self-employment, and the youngsters from well-to-do families too should take up an LIC agency as a career. Ms Vidhu Verma was RM (CC) with me. She liked the idea and asked an advertising agency to develop a script. We finalized it and the short ten minute film was ready. We engaged only TV artists in the film except one which was me. I featured in the film explaining the benefits of an LIC agency. The film was quite catchy. The project was completed in a month's time and we got the CD released at the hands of Mr D K Mehrotra, Chairman LIC. We named it 'LIC Agent *Bano: Ek Unchi Udan*'. It was well appreciated by the DOs/CLIAs and the marketing officials. We then posted it on YouTube, so that it was easily accessible to everyone – even from the remotest corner of the country. Till now over one lakh viewers have viewed it on YouTube.

Kaustubh had turned twenty-six. It was the right age for his marriage. He was initially not ready but Nilambari convinced him to enrol his name on a matrimonial site. We started getting proposals for Kaustubh and in a few months his marriage was fixed with Saylee Khole, an IT engineer, working in Infosys, Pune. The wedding ceremony was performed in Pune on 26 February 2012. Nilambari heaved a sigh of relief!

Tai and Sudhir along with her father-in-law aged over ninety years had come to meet us and stay with us for a week in Delhi. We decided to go to Mathura to visit the Krishna Temples. After visiting the temples and having lunch at Mathura, while we were on our way to Delhi, I got a phone call from Ms Kiran Sahdev RM (P&IR) informing me about the suicide of Mr Laxman Meena, faculty member, Sales Training Centre, Ajmer. She also informed me that the suicide note which he had left was in the possession of the Police and that she had asked SDM Ajmer to arrange a copy and fax it to her. I had never met Mr Meena, nor had I ever spoken to him on telephone.

The next day when I reached office, I saw the copy of the suicide note of Mr Laxman Meena which was faxed by the SDM Ajmer. I was stunned to read my name in the suicide note. It was a one and a half page note on a scribbling pad. It was in Hindi, the extract of which is as follows: "Mr Nilesh Sathe, Zonal Manager, on instigation of Mr K P Choudhary, is going to initiate action against me. I am being trapped although I bear a good character. I am depressed and hence I am committing suicide." It also had a mention of an incident which happened on 4 February 2011 in Delhi. Actually, on that date, I was working in the Central Office, in Mumbai and I had come to know of the incident only on taking charge as Zonal Manager, after Mr V K Sinha retired in June 2011.

What had happened on 4 February 2011?

Mr Laxman Meena was appointed by the then ZM, Mr V K Sinha on the interview committee as a member for promotion of Assistants to Higher Grade Assistants. Since the interviews were to be held for several days, a room in LIC guest house in Janpath was booked for him. A few flats in the same building were occupied by some officers as well.

A couple of days before the interviews were to end, Mr Meena returned to the guest house late at night probably after watching a movie in a theatre. A woman followed him to the guest house and started shouting and demanding money. The caretaker and the watchman prevented her from entering the guest house. She started shouting again and accusing the person who entered the guest house as "he used me and is now refusing to pay me for his enjoyment". This area is famous for such women and incidents of following gentlemen into residential areas and then demanding or extracting money from them were not uncommon. Incidentally, a Police patrolling van was passing by. Hearing a woman shouting, the Police came to check what the commotion was all about. Based on the oral complaint of the woman, they picked up Mr Laxman Meena and took him to the Police station for interrogation.

Mr K P Choudhary, Administrative Officer of LIC was staying in the same building. He was the General Secretary of one of the two SC/ST Associations. Actually, it was called 'Choudhary Group' while the other was 'Shinde Group'. Hearing the noise, Mr Choudhary came to the guest house to see what had happened. When he learnt that the police had taken Mr Meena to the Police station, he made use of his good offices and helped Mr Meena get released from the Police station.

The caretaker and the watchman submitted a letter to ZM, LIC informing him about the incident that happened in the night to which the Personnel Department had put up a note to Mr V K Sinha, ZM, to take necessary action.

After the interviews were over, Mr Meena left for Ajmer without informing LIC about the incident. Had he actually been detained for a day by the Police, conducting interviews on the next day would have been a problem. The Zonal Manager therefore deemed it fit to call for his explanation on why he didn't report the incident to the office and also put his decision on the note submitted by the Personnel Department to get a copy of the FIR from the concerned Police station where he was reported to have been detained that night. He also advised to assign this work to the empanelled advocate of LIC.

The said file was submitted to me only in July 2011 after the retirement of Mr Sinha. I went through the file and observed that there was no progress in the matter for the last four months except a few reminders to Mr Meena as well as to the empanelled advocate. Mr Meena was sent a copy of the letter submitted by the caretaker and the watchman and was asked about the veracity of the incident mentioned by them. There was a letter from Mr Meena in the file asking for some more time to reply. When he received a reminder he had replied, "I am not connected with the incident." He had however not denied that he was taken to the Police station. Hence, I put up my observation on the note "Get a confirmation from Mr Meena that he was not taken to the Police station that night and if at all he was picked up by Police, as reported by the caretaker and the watchman, what action the Police had taken against him."

Accordingly, a letter was sent on 30 August 2011 to Mr Meena and as his reply was not received, a reminder was sent on 26 September 2011 by the personnel department. Even the advocate had not submitted any document from the Police station. When the note was submitted to me at this stage, I wrote, "Advise the advocate to submit his report within eight days, and in case the Police were not co-operating with him, he should inform us accordingly." This yielded results. The advocate submitted a report that there was no FIR lodged against Mr Meena in the concerned Police station. When a note was submitted to me on 29 October 2011 giving the present position, I closed the file with my remarks "the caretaker and the watchman are the employees of the contractor while Mr Laxman Meena is a responsible officer of LIC. As such I believe in the explanation of Mr Meena and the matter is treated as closed exonerating Mr Meena of all the charges in connection with the incident reported by the caretaker and the watchman."

I handed over the file to Ms Kiran Sahdev, RM (P&IR) and advised her to inform Mr Meena on telephone that the file has been closed, to which she said, "Sir, we don't have a practice of communicating the decisions to the employee over phone. If we do it in this case, we may have to inform to every such employee in the future and in case, we fail to do so even once, we may be charged of discrimination. In this Zone, the unions are always on the lookout as to how to trap us." I said, "Okay, then at least ensure that the letter is sent quickly." She agreed and left. That year 30 October was a Sunday and the letter which was dispatched on 31 October, reached him on 3 November but unfortunately on the night of 2November itself, he committed suicide. On 3 November 2011 when Ms Kiran Sahdev informed me of the suicide over phone while I was on my way back from Mathura to Delhi, I felt extremely sad. I felt that had she agreed to my suggestion of informing Mr Meena on telephone on 29 October itself that his case was closed, a suicide could have probably been avoided. It was an unfortunate incident.

When I reached office on 4 November 2011 I went through the suicide note which was written in Hindi in about hundred and fifty words and had Mr Meena's signature. It said, "Zonal Manager, Mr Nilesh Sathe on instigation from Mr K P Choudhary, charge-sheeted me on 30 August 2011 and 26 September 2011 on fake charges due to which I am feeling helpless. A woman followed me to the guest house on 4 February 2011, did so at the instance of K P Choudhary who wanted to blackmail me. The woman's demand for money and calling me bad names was also on the instigation of K P Choudhary. Even the letter of the caretaker and the watchman were written at the instance of K P Choudhary. Due to these incidents, I had to undergo mental stress and physical strain. Due to these false charges, I am feeling frustrated."

My colleagues read it. They suspected that Mr K P Choudhary might be blackmailing him as mentioned by him in the suicide note. I was also informed that Mr Laxman Meena was a good officer and was taken on the interview committee since he was not an active member of any SC/ST Association. Some said that in order to get the Assistants close to Mr K P Choudhary promoted, he might have used some tactics of blackmailing Mr Meena during his stay in the Delhi Guest House. Some of the officers even said, "He may be blackmailing Mr Meena with a threat that he would influence the ZM to impose punishment in the said case. He might have even taken/ demanded money from Mr Meena under the false pretext that he will have to bribe you to close the case." Although Mr K P Choudhary pleaded ignorance when he met me, I too had an inkling of some dubious role played by him as his name was mentioned four times in the suicide note.

Meanwhile, on 5 November 2011 an FIR was filed in the Ajmer Police station against me and Mr K P Choudhary under section 306 and 120(B) - Abetment to suicide. The next day the Police were forced to add Section 3(2)(5) of SC/ST Atrocities Act, probably after learning that I was not from the backward class. Once a case is registered under SC/ST Atrocities Act, the person registered under the offence is denied anticipatory bail. It is a non-bailable offence. Only High Courts are empowered to issue bail.

The Chairman, Mr D K Mehrotra, was informed about the progress of the case daily. On the 8 November 2011 Mr Ajay Singh, IPS, ACP of Ajmer informed me that he was appointed as the investigating officer and would visit my office in Delhi on 9 November 2011 to collect documents and evidence in connection with the case. When he actually came, one Mr Anil Tanwar was with him. Mr Ajay Singh informed me that Mr Tanwar was his friend. Mr Tanwar gave me his visiting card which only had his mobile number. I was a bit surprised to find the ACP bringing his friend to my office but the mystery was unravelled later. Mr Tanwar was only a silent spectator to the proceedings of the meeting held in my cabin.

Mr Ajay Singh asked for the certified copies of all the papers right from the note approving the appointment of Mr Laxman Meena on the interview committee to the letter exonerating him in the case. He called the caretaker and the watchman as well and interrogated them. He also questioned Mr K P Choudhary and Ms Kiran Sahdev, the RM (P&IR). Mr Ajay Singh discussed with me the role of Mr K P Choudhary in the case and said that he would investigate the case in his own way. He left at about 6:00 pm and after finishing my work in the office, I left at around 7:00 pm. While I was on my way home, I got a call on my mobile from Mr Ajay Singh informing me that he had picked up Mr K P Choudhary from his residence at Janpath for investigation and he was being taken to Ajmer Police Station. He also told me that he would keep me posted on further developments at Ajmer.

I immediately informed Mr D K Mehrotra, Chairman, about the recent developments.

I was a bit tense when I reached home. I have a habit of reading a few pages of a book before going to bed but that night it was different. Though I tried reading a book, the contents were not getting registered. My mind was in turmoil. I could not sleep the whole night.

SDM Ajmer of LIC was keeping me posted on developments in the matter. He informed me on 10 November 2011 that Mr K P Choudhary had been arrested and the court had given orders that he should be in Police custody for fifteen days. Mr K P Choudhary had moved the matter to get bail in the case pleading that the provisions of the SC/ST Atrocities Act did not apply to him since he himself belonged to the SC category.

The SDM Ajmer was in regular touch with the Ajmer Police and was keeping me updated on a daily basis. Mr Ajay Singh, ACP was also talking to me occasionally asking for some clarification or the other, about the papers which he had carried back with him. One day he informed me on the phone that the local Meena community leaders met the SP and asked him the reason that in the same case when one accused was arrested, why the other was not yet arrested. I did not smell anything fishy in the conversation I had with Mr Ajay Singh till such time when he called me on 20 November 2011 which was a Sunday. He said, "Mr Sathe, pressure on me is mounting. I may have to summon you to Ajmer

Police Station any time. I would suggest you contact Mr Tanwar immediately. I cannot speak now on the phone."

I knew that the Police generally issue summons for your presence but once you reach the Police station, you are arrested. Knowing this, I told him that I may consult our lawyers before presenting myself to the Ajmer Police. He again insisted that I should contact Mr Tanwar. When I hung up the phone, I realized that Mr Tanwar must be the middleman to manage bribes. The situation was getting quite serious. I asked Neeraj Agrawal, RM (CRM) who was next in the hierarchy for the discharge of official duties in the Zone, Kiran Sahdev and Navin Kaul, RM (Legal) to come to the office. I also reached the office. My PA, Ramesh Chandra was also there. When I told them about the telephone call, they concurred with my inference that Mr Tanwar may be acting as a tout for accepting bribes. We called up the Chairman, Mr Mehrotra to apprise him of the latest developments. He advised me, "Mr Sathe, you go into hiding somewhere in Delhi. Just don't go to Ajmer now. Don't accept summons even if it is issued. Inform only Mr Neeraj and Ms Navin about your whereabouts. Proceed on leave and handover charge to Mr Neeraj. We are consulting our solicitors and are trying to move the matter to Jaipur High Court to see that bail can be arranged for you."

I did as instructed by him. I came home and discussed with Nilambari about where in Delhi, I could hide. The first name that came to our mind was that of Ravi Khare, our next door neighbour in Shankar Nagar, Nagpur, who was working in Delhi for many years. I gave him a call and told him that I might be required to stay in his house, hiding my identity for a month or so if it was not inconvenient for them. I asked him to consult his wife Purva and call me thereafter. He said, "Nilesh, Purva never objects to my decision. You may come any time and stay with us for as many days as you want without any hesitation." I packed a bag with a few clothes, took the file containing copies of the papers relating to the case and reached his place in the evening. I shared his address and contact details with Neeraj, Ramesh Chandra, my PA and

Navin Kaul and removed my SIM card from the mobile so that I become unreachable on phone.

Every evening, Neeraj used to inform me of all the important events of the day. Just the next day after I went into hiding, he informed me that Mr Ajay Singh had called. He wanted to know my whereabouts and enquired whether I had contacted Mr Tanwar. He also indicated to Neeraj that if I didn't approach Mr Tanwar, an arrest warrant would be issued in my name. To all these threats, Neeraj kept on telling him that he held the charge of ZM in my absence and if he needed any official documents or clarification, he was ready to give them.

In the meanwhile, some papers were sent to me for signature regarding 'Vakalatnama' in favour of Advocate Raj Singh Bajwa of Jaipur High Court. Advocate Bajwa also had a word with me and advised me not to contact Mr Tanwar at any cost, since he appeared to be a tout for exchange of money. Within a week thereafter, the case was filed in Jaipur High Court. Advocate Bajwa informed me that the case was likely to be heard on 29 November 2011 and the grant of bail was expected by 5 December 2011. I was happy. But to my dismay, the Police Prosecutor, under some pretext or the other, kept on dragging the case till 8 December 2011. To my misfortune, just a day before the case was posted for the final hearing and judgement, on the night of 7 December 2011 Advocate Bajwa died of a massive cardiac arrest. Hearing this, the Judge, Mr Sharma, instead of posting the case after a week, posted it only on 7 January 2012 after the winter vacations.

There was no point in continuing to stay with Ravi Khare any longer. Already eighteen days had passed. I decided to shift to my sister's place in Nagpur. Tai and Sudhir were in the know of things. They also advised me to stay with them in Dharampeth, Nagpur, instead of staying somewhere else. I left Delhi on 8 December 2011 by a late evening flight to Nagpur. After being in Nagpur, I did not have much to worry as Sudhir, my sister's husband, being Chief Editor of Tarun Bharat, Nagpur, a leading daily, had lots of connections in public life.

As it is, it was winter, so I used to cover my face with a monkey cap or a muffler and go out for a walk in the morning and in the evening. One of my colleagues from LIC, Mr Sudhakar Ingole, who stayed in a flat in the same campus, later learnt of my stay there for over a month, said, "It's surprising how I didn't notice you for such a long period!" I didn't visit any of our relatives or acquaintances in Nagpur except Nilambari's mother who stayed at a walking distance in Laxmi Nagar and to a doctor for my medical treatment.

While in Delhi, occasionally I used to pass blood through my rectum at the time of passing of stools. The Medical Referee of LIC from Delhi was giving me some medicines, but the bleeding didn't stop completely. Of late, when I was in Nagpur, the frequency of bleeding went up. I got worried and met Dr Pravin Gupta, a piles specialist in Nagpur who gave me some medicines and said, "With these medicines too, if the oozing of blood doesn't stop, we may have to operate on the piles." I informed my brother-like friend, Dr Ashok Deshpande, who lived in Sangli. He knew Dr Gupta since his college days. In spite of the medicines given by Dr Gupta, the bleeding did not stop. I went to him again and connected him to Dr Ashok Deshpande who advised him to check by inserting his finger in the rectum if any polyp was felt. He did accordingly and when he informed Dr Deshpande of a polyp, he asked Dr Gupta to refer me to Dr Arvind Joglekar, a surgeon, for further consultation.

Accordingly, I met Dr Joglekar the next day. He examined me and confirmed the existence of a polyp about 10 cm from the mouth of rectum. He advised me to go to Dr Abhiram Paranjape, gastroenterologist for a biopsy. He also said that if the biopsy report indicated non-malignant polyp, he would operate it but if it was malignant, he would advise me to see an onco-surgeon.

The, biopsy was done on 12 January 2012. I was regularly informing Nilambari about the case and my health condition. She was also keeping me updated on the moves of Ajay Singh. Mr K P Choudhary, in the meanwhile, was released on bail, after being in Police custody for fifteen days. He informed Nilambari over the phone to keep a substantial amount ready to bribe the Police officer since he too had spent a good amount for getting released from police custody. Nilambari told him that her husband was not guilty and had done no wrong and as such there was no question of bribing anyone. He still kept on insisting, "I will still advise you to set aside ₹5 to ₹10 lakh for bribing without which it's impossible for Mr Sathe to keep himself away from the clutches of the police." He even visited our bungalow in Sundar Nagar two or three times to convince Nilambari to keep the bribe amount ready. Finally, Nilambari told him sternly, "Mr Choudhary, I have told you earlier and now I am telling you once and for all that we are not going to bribe anyone. Let the law take its own course. We are ready to face any legal consequences, but we won't do anything that is illegal." Only after hearing such stern words from Nilambari did he stop visiting or speaking to her.

In the meanwhile, Nilambari had gone to Pune to attend the wedding of Madhumita Sarkhel's daughter, our family friend and my office colleague. Lot of my friends and senior officers had come for the wedding. Those who were knowing about me going into hiding, asked her, "How long will he hide from the Police?" When she told them about K P Choudhary's suggestion, they also assured her to raise the required funds for the bribe. My friend Mr Milind Mane similarly assured her that he would raise the amount in no time. One of them further said, "I won't be surprised if K P Choudhary has promised Mr Ajay Singh to extract the bribe from you and in the process, might have gotten some discount in the amount he paid to Ajay Singh for his own release." Nilambari thanked all of them but asserted that bribing a Police officer was against our principles and she would never do so.

One day, when I called her from Nagpur, already more than fifty days had passed since I went into hiding. I told her, "Nilambari, I am not sure how many more days I may have to be in hiding. How long will the Chairman of LIC leave the position of ZM Delhi vacant? If he posts someone in my place, you may have to vacate the Sundar Nagar bungalow. Are you prepared to face a situation like this?" She boldly replied, "You don't worry, I am ready to face any situation but don't bribe any one, for I know that you are innocent and no crime has been committed by you, I won't pay a single rupee bribe to anyone. If the Chairman posts someone in your place, I will take a house in Gurugram on rent and vacate the bungalow and shift into the rented house with Kaustubh immediately. I have no attraction for the LIC bungalow in Delhi."

I was moved, looking at her courage and hearing her words of determination, I felt proud to have such a wife. But the fact remains that those days were very tough. But as it is said, 'When the going gets tough, the tough gets going'. The next day Ms Navin Kaul, RM (Legal) informed me that LIC had decided to move to Supreme Court seeking relief for me and she was advised to meet and engage a well-known Supreme Court lawyer, Advocate KTS Tulsi for filing a case in the Supreme Court. I felt happy that my institution, LIC, was supporting me and had implicit faith in me.

Ms Navin Kaul met Advocate KTS Tulsi who, after hearing the details of the case and going through the papers asked her, "If the Supreme Court asks you why you didn't seek relief from District and Sessions' Court, Ajmer, what justification do you have?" Ms Navin replied, "Sir, can we not take a stand that the authority to grant bail in such cases, vests only with the High Court and hence we didn't move the matter in the lower court of Ajmer."

"Why do you presume? As it is, there is still some time for the Courts to reopen after the winter holidays. In the meanwhile, let us seek relief from Ajmer District Court when it opens on 12 January 2012. We shall request the Court to hear it on priority."

What he said was quite logical. Accordingly, the case was filed by Advocate Vivek Bajwa, the son of the deceased Advocate Raj Singh Bajwa, as per the advice of Advocate KTS Tulsi. It was effectively pleaded in the plaint that as Mr Sathe is in charge of North Zone of LIC, he is a senior officer in the rank of ED. The action taken by

Mr Sathe against the deceased officer was only in his official capacity. He had not seen, met or spoken with Mr Meena. As such the action of the Police in charging him under Atrocities Act is ultra-vires and as such, the relevant sections be invoked and an anticipatory bail be granted to him on proper terms.

The case was admitted on 12 January 2012 and was posted for arguments on 16 January 2012. The judgement was delivered on the same day. The date on which my case was admitted in the Ajmer court, coincided with the date when Dr Abhiram Paranjape conducted the biopsy of the tumour, in Nagpur. The biopsy report was to be received after eight days. Both these decisions were going to be crucial in my life. We always wish that only good things should take place in our lives. Naturally, I wished that the Ajmer Court should grant me anticipatory bail and the biopsy report should state that the tumour was non-malignant.

I was eagerly waiting a call from Ms Navin Kaul on 16 January 2012 to know the outcome of the case in the Ajmer Court. Finally, at about 3:00 pm, she called me and was very excited to inform me that the Court had granted me anticipatory bail. She said, "Sir, what happened on 16 January 2012 in Ajmer Court was never heard of. The courtroom was jam packed to hear the arguments of Advocate KTS Tulsi. He forcefully but logically put forth his arguments as to why Atrocities Act was not applicable in this case as Mr Sathe had not seen, met or spoken with Mr Meena and submitted to the Court, variety of case laws to substantiate that what Mr Sathe did was in his official capacity in discharge of his duties. His act cannot be termed as atrocity which involves wicked, cruel act, typically involving physical violence or injury. Charging him under the Atrocities Act by Police is hence, untenable. Mr Sathe, hence be awarded anticipatory bail..."

The Police Prosecutor vehemently opposed the grant of bail. He brought it to the notice of the Court that there was no provision for granting anticipatory bail under Atrocities Act. He said, "It's a non-bailable offence and as such the case should be dismissed without giving any relief, whatsoever to Mr Sathe."

The Judge was annoyed. He asked the Police Prosecutor, "Will you explain why the Police charged Mr Sathe of Atrocities when he did not see, meet or speak with the deceased person, Mr Meena? You will charge people under the wrong sections of the Act to harass them and will then plead that no anticipatory bail be given. This is incorrect." And he granted me anticipatory bail with the condition that I should present myself before the Police and cooperate with them and I should not leave the country. It was clear that the Ajmer Police could not arrest me and I had no threat from Mr Ajay Singh anymore. I called and thanked Advocate Vivek Bajwa, who advised me to rejoin duties in Delhi. It was a big relief. I took the blessings of Tai and Sudhir and left by the late evening flight to Delhi to join on Saturday, the 17 January 2012.

All my colleagues were happy to meet me after a gap of fifty-six days. On 19 January 2012 there was a Business Review Meeting scheduled in Mumbai, for which I left on 18 January. The biopsy report was likely to be received on 19 January. Sudhir went to Dr Moghe's Pathological Lab in the evening on 19 January to find that the report was ready. He collected it and called me and said, "Nilesh, the report indicates malignancy. I am sending you the report by email. I suggest you seek an appointment of an oncologist in Mumbai."

When Sudhir called, my meeting was over and I was waiting for the staff car to leave for my residence in Kalina, Santacruz. I asked the driver to wait for a while and went to meet the Chairman, Mr Mehrotra. I informed him of the biopsy report. He advised me to get the operation done in Mumbai. He was kind enough to reassure me not to worry about the business of North Zone but to attend to my health condition and recover quickly. I met the other two MDs, Mr Mathew T and Mr A K Dasgupta as well. In the meanwhile, I spoke with Dr Ashok Deshpande. I had sent him the report in an email. He went through it and he told me that he would take an appointment with Dr Raman Deshpande, onco-surgeon, attached to Raheja Hospital.

On my way back home to Kalina, I called up Nilambari to inform her about the biopsy report and told her that Himanshu would book her flight tickets to Mumbai for the next day. I advised her to be ready to stay in Mumbai for two to three weeks. I also informed my PA., Mr Ramesh Chandra, about the malignancy and that I won't be able to join office for the next two to three weeks. By the time I reached Kalina, I got a call from Dr Ashok Deshpande informing me that an appointment with Dr Raman Deshpande was confirmed for 10:00 am on 20 January 2012.

Himanshu sent tickets to Nilambari and he took leave for a week. Nilambari reached Mumbai by the evening flight on the same day. Tai and Sudhir also came from Nagpur to assist her. We met Dr Raman Deshpande. He saw the biopsy report and other reports and drew a diagram explaining to us the location of the malignant polyp. He said, "In order to find the exact location of the polyp, we will need a PET CT Scan. It will also indicate if the cancer has spread anywhere else in the body." He also prescribed blood tests, ECG, chest X-ray, etc. He further said, "Mr Sathe, let me alert you that in case the position of the polyp is at a distance of less than 10 cms or 4 inches from the anal opening, I will be ruthless in removing your rectum. Himanshu had his question ready, he asked, "Doctor, in that case will he have an artificial rectum?" Doctor smiled and said, "We give an opening in the stomach (called stoma) and fix to it a colostomy bag which is a plastic bag where the excreta is collected. That bag will have to be cleaned regularly."

Taking his prescription for the tests, we left the hospital and reached home. We had to prepare psychologically and financially. The next day, we went to various hospitals and pathological labs to get the tests done. Himanshu made all the appointments and by the time we reached home, it was 2:00 pm. He asked me to rest and picked up the reports in the evening.

When he brought the reports, we went through them out of curiosity. We realized that hemoglobin, triglyceride, cholesterol, HDL, LDL, ECG were all within normal limits. X-ray of chest was clear but the PET CT did make a mention of metastasis which was localised to the rectum.

On 22 January 2012 we met Dr Deshpande with the reports. He said, "Mr Sathe, the good news is that the cancer has not spread anywhere else in the body and the polyp is more than 12 cms from the anal opening, and as such, in all probabilities, I may be able to save the rectum, although I won't guarantee it." It was a big relief for us. He further asked me, "Mr Sathe, surgery is a must but if you want to take a second opinion, you may do so. If you want to check an auspicious day for the surgery or for admission, you may do so and meet me next week if you want me to operate on you."

I never believed in the concept of 'auspicious day'. I believed that each day that Almighty has given us, is an 'auspicious day'. There is no need to refer to almanac. Moreover, as my friend Dr Ashok Deshpande had referred me to Dr Raman Deshpande, there was no reason to take a second opinion. I asked him, "Doctor, how quickly can we finalize the date of surgery? I want you to perform the surgery." He checked with the hospital administration about availability of the operation theatre, anesthesiologist, etc. and asked me to get admitted the same evening. The operation was scheduled to be performed the very next day. He asked us to contact the admission staff on the ground floor for the estimate of expenses, payment of advance etc. We were told that the estimated expenses for surgery and a ten day stay in the hospital would cost about ₹7 lakh, if we wanted a single occupancy room and ₹4 lakh if we opted for a room on a twin sharing room. The Group Mediclaim Policy of LIC had a cover of ₹3 lakh for my cadre. Hence we decided to settle on twin sharing room. Himanshu paid advance through his credit cards and there began my fight with cancer.

I got admitted to the hospital the same evening. Himanshu was to stay with me that night. When at night, I was trying to sleep, the ever-daunting question which comes to the mind of every cancer patient came to my mind too. “Why me?” I never smoked; I was not addicted to any vices. My eating habits were moderate. I used to go for a brisk morning walk of five kilometres daily. I used to exercise regularly. Despite all these good habits, “Why me?”

Was it out of stress? Had the stress of my fifty-six days of hiding out impacted my health? Was cancer hereditary? My mother’s mother died of cancer, my mother died of cancer which is it going to be my turn now? I read a lot of literature on cancer on the Internet. It helped me learn more about cancer which reduced the fear in my mind to some extent. It also helped me ask appropriate questions to the surgeon before the surgery. I did not suffer from fear-psychosis. I read that cancer is not incurable, so I was determined to say to myself that my cancer will be cured. I will be cancer free. Did I delay in consulting a doctor? No, but probably the line of treatment for the last six months aimed at treating piles might have been wrong. But I did consult doctors, I did not ignore the problem.

Was ‘Meena’ case a blessing in disguise? Probably yes. Because had I been in Delhi, I might not have taken my illness seriously. I was so busy in office work that I might have ignored it or postponed the consultation with the surgeon. It was only because I was in Nagpur and had lot of time that I paid serious attention to my health condition. It reinforced my conviction that whatever happens, happens for the good.

I thought to myself how God was kind to me! I got the anticipatory bail just a few days before the surgery. How difficult would it have been for me to get the surgery done if I was in hiding? God was always kind to me and the blessings of my mother would steer me out of these difficult times, I reiterated to myself. I don’t know when I slept but it was a sound sleep and I got up only at 6:00 am when a nurse came to remind me not to eat anything and get ready for the surgery.

Before I was taken to the operation theatre, Nilambari, Tai, Sudhir, Himanshu, Kaustubh, and a few friends had come to see me. At 8:30 am I was taken to the operation theatre. The anesthesiologist asked me to sit with my legs near my chest, told me that she would be giving me injections through my spine, encouraged me not to worry and reassured me that the surgery would be successful and within a minute, I lost consciousness.

I was operated on 23 January 2012 then shifted to the Intensive Care Unit (ICU) for twenty-four hours. When I was in the ICU, I remember that I had opened my eyes and I had seen Nilambari standing next to me. I asked her in feeble voice and gestured to ask if the rectum was saved. She whispered, "Rectum is saved." After that I went into deep slumber. Finally, when the effect of anesthesia wore off, I woke up and was moved from the ICU to the twin-sharing room. When I stabilized, I realized that I had a tube through my nose, two more tubes were attached to my stomach along with a catheter. I also noticed that a plastic bag was attached below my right lung which Nilambari informed me was a colostomy bag attached to the stoma, a makeshift arrangement to pass stools, to enable the healing of the rectum post surgery.

When I opened my eyes, I found a board hanging to the saline stand near my bed with letters 'NBM'. I thought that it was a mistake. My initials are NBS hence I asked Nilambari to ask the nurse to correct it. She laughed and said, it has nothing to do with my initials but meant, 'Nil By Mouth' which means, even by mistake, nobody should feed me anything by mouth, not even water. I laughed to realize that my throat was dry. I swallowed a bit of saliva and I felt better.

Initially, for a couple of days, someone or the other was always there with me in the hospital. Nilambari invariably used to be there at night. The first few days in the hospital were quite critical. The patient on the other bed in the room must have been in severe pain. Throughout the night, he was moaning and crying. The patient's attendant had to sleep on the floor. There was no bed or a cot for the attendant to rest. I felt bad finding Nilambari sleeping on the floor on a mattress. On the third day, when I gained full consciousness, I asked Himanshu to enquire if we may be allotted a separate single occupancy room. He came back to inform me of a rule, which I had never heard of. He said, "The administrative staff informed me that even if you are shifted to a single room today, they will charge us for a single room right from the day you got admitted and not from the day of shifting to a single occupancy room. We shall have to pay the operation charges, visiting fees etc. as are applicable to a single room although when you were operated, you were in a twin sharing room!" It was ridiculous but was followed by all the hospitals. In short, we had to keep ₹7 lakh ready if we wanted a single occupancy room. Even the visiting fees of the doctors increase in proportion to different room-occupancy categories.

Nilambari said, "It's only a matter of a few more days. I will manage, you don't worry." After three days, the 'NBM' board was removed and I was allowed to have a light diet and liquids. The physiotherapy followed. Friends and relatives started pouring in during visiting hours. I started reading emails and replying to them from my iPad. My routine was getting set and I was feeling better. The only problem was that I was experiencing acute pain in the abdomen. I had not passed any stools. The colostomy bag attached was absolutely dry. When I enquired with the nurse, she said, "As it is, you have not eaten much, it would take some time for the excreta to collect in the bag." Finally, on the fourth day, when the house surgeon was on visit, I told him about my uneasiness and non-collection of excreta in the colostomy bag. He examined me and found that the bag was incorrectly attached. He called the concerned nurse, fired her, took me to OPD and fixed the colostomy bag to the abdomen properly. Soon, excreta started flowing in the bag and the pain in my abdomen subsided.

My recovery was quite good. One after the other, the tubes from nose and abdomen were removed. I became quite mobile thereafter. My initial diet was only soups and juices which changed to regular food from the seventh day onward. The catheter was the last to leave my body. I was asked to walk as much as possible which I followed meticulously. I noticed that my weight had reduced substantially and when I walked even fifty steps at one go, I felt exhausted. Those were the most challenging days for Nilambari but she never grumbled about any inconvenience, including having to sleep on the floor near my bed at night. I could observe Himanshu's discomfort on seeing his mother's inconvenience. One day he said, "I am such a junior officer in my company but even for me, the Mediclaim limit is ₹5 lakh. It appears to be ridiculous that an ED level Officer in LIC has a Mediclaim limit of only ₹3 lakh." I had no answer but one day, while I was checking my emails, I came across an email written by Himanshu to my dear friend S K Roy who was then the Zonal Manager of Eastern Zone, copied to me. On reading it, I felt proud of him and realized how hurt he was due to the inconvenience faced by his mother. He wrote:

Respected Sir,

I am Himanshu, son of your friend Nilesh Sathe.

I am beginning this letter as 'Sir' and not 'Uncle' because I am going to mention a policy matter of LIC which I feel needs your urgent attention.

As you are already aware, my Dad had to undergo an urgent cancer surgery. As he was unwell, I was taking care of his hospitalization procedure and expenses and I want to share my concern about the Mediclaim Policy which LIC has for its employees.

1. When the doctor informed me that urgent surgery was required, I wanted my Dad to get the best facilities so that he recovers quickly and his stay in the hospital is as comfortable as possible.
2. Upon enquiry, we found that the room rent and the surgery cost for a single occupancy room was ₹7 lakh while the cost of a twin sharing room and surgery was about ₹4 lakh. The hospital was Raheja and not Hinduja or Breach Candy where

the cost would have been even higher. The twin sharing room had no provision of abed for the attendant to rest at night and the stream of visitors was bound to disturb the other patient in the sharing room, so I wanted a single occupancy room.

3. I was quite sure that being an Executive Director of one of the biggest insurers of the world, his Mediclaim would cover the cost of a single private room. But I was aghast to find that an ED of India's Insurance behemoth is entitled to only ₹3 lakh Mediclaim cover!!! Isn't it the height of irony that the organization which wants customers to get proper insurance for themselves because insurance can never be enough, gives a meagre ₹3 lakh Mediclaim for its employees in the highest cadre! I also found out that there was no provision for the employees to increase the sum assured of the Mediclaim by choosing to pay a higher premium on his own.
4. It also amazed me that there was no cashless facility as a result of which we had to pay the entire amount in cash/ cards, because cheque payment was not allowed.
5. After looking at the cost and arranging so much cash in such a short time, I had to unwillingly admit him to a twin sharing room. I feel sorry that my Mom has been sleeping on the floor, though without any complaint as there is no cot and bed facility available for the attendant in the twin sharing room. Neither my Dad nor my Mom have grumbled even once about this, but I am feeling sorry for them, hence this email.

Today we are going through these testing times but tomorrow it could be anyone else. I would humbly request you to take up the issue of increasing the limit under the Mediclaim Policy for Executive Directors to at least ₹10 lakh and a cashless facility should also be provided. I trust you will take appropriate decisions in this regard at the proper time.

Regards,
Himanshu (son of Nilesh Sathe)

Later, when S K Roy became Chairman, LIC, the first thing he did was to increase the Mediclaim limit for all employees substantially. I won't say that it was only due to Himanshu's letter but the fact remains that he increased the Mediclaim limit soon after becoming Chairman.

While reading Himanshu's email, I had tears of satisfaction in my eyes. I felt proud to have him as my son who took the inconvenience of his parents to heart and wrote about it to a Senior Officer of LIC.

I was discharged from hospital on 2 February 2012. I moved to Himanshu's flat in Kalina. The stitches were removed on 8 February 2012 and Dr Raman Deshpande allowed me to join the office after three weeks of surgery, on 13 February 2012. Accordingly, I joined my services in Delhi.

While I was hiding out in Nagpur, I had called Mr Diwakar Khole, father of Kaustubh's bride, Saylee, to meet me. This was to give him first-hand information about the 'Meena' case I was facing. When he came, he began discussing the topic of fixing the wedding date. I told him to go ahead and also that in case, I didn't get bail by then, the rituals would be performed either by Tai and Sudhir or by Himanshu and Prajakta. He is a firm believer and an ardent follower of Swami Samarth, from Akkalkot. He gave me a sacred book on Swamiji and advised me to read it daily. He further said, "Swamiji's blessings will surely bring you out safely from these difficult days."

The three bygone months was a testing time for Nilambari. Kaustubh's wedding was fixed on 26 February 2012. In my absence she got Invitation Cards printed, despatched and made purchases for the wedding. I felt sorry for not being of help to her in managing household responsibilities. She had to manage all that single-handedly.

After joining office, I applied for ten days leave from 23 February to 3 March 2012 for Kaustubh's wedding in Pune. The wedding date was 26 February 2012. I was able to attend Kaustubh's wedding; Mr Diwakar Khole's absolute faith in Swami Samarth, thus yielded results. We returned to Delhi after the wedding. They went to Manali for their honeymoon and I joined my office in Jeevan Bharati, Connaught Place, New Delhi.

Going to the office with colostomy bag attached to my abdomen was a great discomfort. I used to regularly carry an extra bag, cleaning material, adhesive tape, dusting powder etc. to the office so that in case the colostomy bag leaked, I would replace it myself. In spite of all such difficulties, I continued going to office and attending meetings and conferences. I had lost over ten kilograms. I was looking slim and trim.

In the meanwhile, I was summoned by Ajmer Police to record my oral evidence. Travelling to Ajmer with a colostomy bag attached to my abdomen was not easy. I went by air to Jaipur and then travelled by car for four hours to reach Ajmer. The ACP who recorded my evidence was not Mr Ajay Singh. On enquiry, I was informed that Mr Ajay Singh was under suspension for some charges. It was in a way good that my statement got recorded in March 2012 because otherwise, I would have had to travel to Ajmer from Mumbai, since in April 2012 I was transferred as Director and CEO of LIC Nomura Mutual Fund Asset Management Company (AMC). In due course the case registered against me in Jaipur High Court was decided in my favour and the judgement was delivered in October 2013 exonerating me of all charges.

Nilambari believed that dormant cancer cells in my body became active due to the stress I had in Meena's case, although my view is different. I believe that human beings have incidents of happiness and sorrows in life. We should not attach reasoning to such incidents. If tobacco leads to cancer, I know about small infants having cancer. If liquor causes cancer, I know a few persons who consumed liquor regularly but lived over the age of eighty. I was away from all such vices and have led a healthy life but despite this I was attacked by cancer. I think we should just take it as an accident. We should never try to find a reason for the same. When you meet with an accident, it is not always due to your fault. What's important is to face the situation with a brave heart. I have this frame of mind which you may call philosophical, but I don't generally lose my balance.

Mr D K Mehrotra, Chairman, had come to Delhi in the first week of April 2012 and was staying in the guest house which was next to my quarters in Sundar Nagar, Delhi. I invited him for breakfast and thanked him for the support he gave me during my difficult days. He replied, "Nilesh I think, a posting in Mumbai may help you take better care of your health." I sensed his intention to shift me to Mumbai which I didn't want. I said, "Sir, I am now cancer-free. I am regaining the lost weight. My first choice would be to continue in the present assignment but in case you intend to shift me to Mumbai, please give me an assignment which is more challenging so that my skills will be tested." He smiled and said, "You may not want to come to Mumbai leaving Delhi in a year but I want you to take charge as Director and CEO of LIC Nomura Mutual Fund Asset Management Company (LIC MF AMC). You know that we partnered with Nomura of Japan a few years ago, but the AUM has plunged from over ₹50,000 crore to just above ₹5,000 crore due to the global meltdown and some other reasons. I want you to head the joint venture and take some bold and drastic steps to bring the AMC back to glory. I am sure that you will like to accept this challenging assignment."

"Sir, although I have no experience of working in the Investment Department or in LIC HFL, I am happy that you chose me for this assignment. I will do my best wherever you post me."

"I know your capability Nilesh. I am sure, you will steer the AMC out of the present crisis situation."

In the next fortnight, orders were issued and I was transferred as Director and CEO of LIC MF AMC, Mumbai. There is a general perception in LIC that a posting in a subsidiary company is a 'sideline' posting. While LIC's Assets Under Management (AUM) was over ₹12 lakh crore, the AUM of its AMC was not even one per cent of it. With your posting in the subsidiary, one is no doubt away from the mainstream and as such, not many accept such a posting with a smile but I was positive. I took it as an opportunity to learn an entirely new line of business about which most of us in LIC have scanty knowledge. I knew that it won't be a cake-walk but I was ready to face the challenges. There were a few Japanese working in the AMC and were holding high positions. I considered it as an opportunity to learn their way of managing business. Rather than cribbing about a side-lined posting, I took it in my stride and took charge of the new assignment within a week of issuance of the order.

We shifted Kaustubh and Saylee to a rented accommodation in Gurugram. Nilambari stayed with them for a couple of days to help them to set up their house and mainly the kitchen. Initially, I stayed in the LIC Guest House at Churchgate, Mumbai, and on getting allotment of quarter at Jeevan Jyot Building on Napean Sea Road, we shifted from Delhi in the last week of May 2012 bidding goodbye to Sundar Nagar, Delhi.

My one year in Delhi gave me two blows, one was professional; the judicial case, while the other was personal; colorectal cancer, but the silver lining was Kaustubh's wedding. We were free from our household responsibilities with both the sons married while I still had five to six more years to retire.

Lessons Learnt...

- Stick to your morals and principles even when the going gets tough. Stand tall with courage and determination.
- Presume nothing.
- Each day that the Almighty has given us is an 'auspicious day'.
- Whatever happens, happens for the good.
- Prayer brings peace to restless heart and mind.
- Your loved ones are pillar of strength in times of trouble, learn to appreciate what they do for you.
- Rather than cribbing over a side-lined posting, take it in your stride and accept the challenge.

X

Learning Curve – LIC Mutual Fund and My Fight with Cancer

I shifted to the spacious four bedroom quarters at Jeevan Jyot, Nepean Sea Road, Mumbai. During high tide, water from the sea used to splash over to the garden of the building over and above the six feet high compound wall. The sound of waves was heard particularly during nights. We often used to enjoy our morning tea, sitting on the balcony facing the sea.

After taking charge as Director and CEO of LIC Nomura Mutual Fund Asset Management Company (LIC AMC), the first thing I did was to find the reasons for the downfall of the AMC from its peak Assets Under Management (AUM) of over ₹50,000 crore to ₹5,400 crore. The main reason which I observed was that although it was a private sector mutual fund with LIC's holding of just thirty-five per cent, it was run like a public sector mutual fund. The employees were entitled to leave, annual increments like LIC employees and salary was not linked to performance. I did SWOT analysis of the company and made a presentation to the LIC Chairman, Mr Mehrotra.

I told him, "Sir, I will need to take some drastic steps to bring the company out of the red. I need your support for the same. Please keep me here for at least three years as it will take quite some time to set things right. I will submit Action Taken Report (ATR) every month to keep you informed of the progress of the AMC since you are the Chairman of LIC AMC as well."

I had to toil hard to make grassroot changes. The Chairman and the Board of Directors always supported me. After three years, when I left the office, the LIC AMC was in the top twenty out of the forty-five AMCs and was one out of the ten showing profits. Assets Under Management (AUM) increased by over one hundred and forty per cent to over ₹13,000 crore. Most of the schemes had started generating alpha over the benchmark indices.

During the initial days of joining the Mumbai office, I stayed in LIC Guest House at Churchgate. My biggest worry was changing the colostomy bag. When I was in Delhi, Nilambari used to help me while changing the bag, but here, I had to do it myself. It had been three months since the surgery and as suggested by Dr Raman Deshpande, it was time to do the corrective surgery of closing the cut on the abdomen taking the large intestine back to its original place and reconnecting it to the rectum. We finalized the date of surgery in Raheja Hospital in the third week of May 2012. All the pre-surgical clinical tests were done. On reviewing the reports, Dr Deshpande was satisfied and asked me to get admitted on 17 May 2012 for the operation to restore rectum.

I was under the impression that it was a simple corrective surgery but Dr Deshpande clarified to me, "Mr Sathe, no surgery is simple." Our Mediclaim limits were revised by then and as such I could occupy a single occupancy room. It took four hours to perform the surgery. I was in the ICU for a day and on regaining consciousness, I was shifted to the room. Tai and Sudhir had come from Nagpur to support Nilambari. Since I was CEO, I had a staff car for personal use as well. It was of great help for the family members to make visits to the hospital. There were twelve stitches to the abdomen where the colostomy bag was fitted earlier. A port was implanted near the neck to avoid pushing a needle through a vein every time for injecting medicine. As a result, my hands were free to move. The 'NBM' board was kept hanging for the first three days and removed later when I was allowed to have soups and a liquid diet. A tube was attached to the abdomen for clearing the oozing blood from the body. To drain the urine without exertion, a catheter was inserted.

On the sixth day, when it was observed that the out-flow of blood had totally stopped from the tube attached to the abdomen, the house surgeon decided to remove it. He applied some cream, maybe some anesthetic lotion on the skin around the tube and pulled it. Unfortunately, some portion of the tube remained inside the body. Again, local anesthesia was given and the remaining part of the tube was removed, for which two more stitches were required. It was quite painful. The house surgeon was either not well versed with his job or the tube had got stuck inside the abdomen more firmly than he expected. But the result was that my stay in the hospital increased by a day. When I asked him about why it happened, he casually replied, "It happens sometimes because the tube gets stuck to the inner body but now, I have done the needful. Don't worry."

His justification appeared to cover up his fault. I called my friend Dr Ashok Deshpande and informed him about it. He said, "It should never happen. Before removing the tube, the doctor should follow a protocol. He should ask the patient to hold his breath and be ready to pull the tube and when the patient releases the breath under pressure, at that moment, the tube should be pulled. Anyway, you are fortunate that he at least admitted that a portion of the tube broke and remained inside and he removed it immediately otherwise it would have led to complications in the future."

During the last three days of my stay in the hospital, a physiotherapist used to visit twice a day. I was given a laxative medicine daily to enable me to pass stools comfortably. I got rid of the colostomy bag and that was a big relief. I came home after being in the hospital for ten days.

Passing of stools was a persistent problem for me after the surgery despite taking the prescribed laxative. When I met Dr Raman Deshpande after eight days for removal of stitches, I told him about the same. He suggested a different laxative with a higher dose. When I started taking it as prescribed, I had to wake up just after four hours of going to bed to pass stools. The dosage was not getting adjusted and the natural passing of stools had become a rare occasion. When I brought it to the notice of Dr Deshpande, he said, "During surgery for colorectal cancer, our focus is on the removal of the tumour with its roots. While doing so, sometimes the tissues which support the rectum to expand and contract, get cut and they can't be restored. You will have to be laxative-dependent for life." As per protocol, a CT scan was done in August 2012 which was normal. I was advised to do a sonography of the abdomen in November 2012.

In the meanwhile, a report of the K-ras Mutation test was received after about three months from my first surgery. I was told that the test was negative, meaning that the cancer that I had was not genetically transmitted. In simple words, there was less possibility of transmission of cancer genetically to the next generation. We were happy to know the meaning of the report. I also consulted two other oncologists to find out if chemotherapy or radiation was required. Both of them were of the view that since it was a first stage cancer and surgery was done, chemotherapy or radiation was not required. Everything was good, except the problem of a dysfunctional rectum which did not allow me to pass stools in a natural way. One gastroenterologist recommended a 'Ballooning Test' which confirmed that the rectum functioning of contraction and expansion was severely impacted and may not get restored. I continued with an increased dose of laxative but finally moved to taking an enema of lukewarm water every morning. It suited me and for the last many years, I am quite at ease and comfortable with it.

The sonography report of November 2012 was normal. But the sonography done three months later indicated metastasis, spread of cancer to the liver. When the radiologist saw the earlier sonography report of November 2012 he said, "Some traces of metastasis are seen here. Your doctor should not have ignored the same." But whatever had to happen, had happened. Dr Raman Deshpande was also surprised and advised me to get CT scan done with liver biopsy, if need be.

Accordingly, I got the tests done at Breach Candy Hospital. It showed that cancer had spread to two out of eight segments of the liver. Dr Raman Deshpande was to suggest the name of a liver surgeon since he himself was not a liver specialist. We were all extremely upset and worried. Himanshu browsed through various sites and we zeroed down on a liver surgeon, Dr Ankur Shah who was attached to Kokilaben Dhirubhai Ambani Hospital (KDAH). Himanshu arranged for an appointment. When we met him, he asked, "Who referred you to me?" Himanshu replied, "Internet" and the surgeon had a big laugh. He said, "The new generation, Mr Sathe, relies more on the internet than on anyone else." He took the biopsy report and CD of the CT scan to a senior surgeon and came back to advise us to get PET CT done to ascertain if the cancer had spread to any other parts of the body or is localized only on the liver.

Accordingly, PET CT was done. Fortunately, cancer had not spread and was localized only to the second and eighth segments of liver. Dr Shah explained to us in detail about how the surgery would be done. He drew a figure of Liver, marked the segments where cancer cells had metastasized and said, "Mr Sathe, I will remove about thirty per cent of your liver. It will be removed just as the ice-cream vendor uses a scoop to take out ice-cream from the ice-cream pot. I will use an electronic gun to remove the affected portion. The positive thing is that liver is the only organ in our body that grows back." Himanshu had searched on the Internet for questions one should ask a surgeon before surgery. Dr Shah replied to all those questions. He gave us sufficient time, explaining the seriousness of the metastasis and what precautions should be taken post-surgery.

The liver cancer surgery was done on 21 March 2013 just thirteen months after the colorectal cancer surgery. This time again, Tai and Sudhir had come to help and support Nilambari. Physical and psychological support is very much required during the days of hospitalization. Fortunately, I had my Tai and brother-in-law who always came to my rescue.

By now, I had become used to the hospital's protocol. I was in ICU for a day and then was moved to a single occupancy room. A port was fixed on my neck for feeding. Two tubes were attached to the abdomen for the oozing blood to come out from the surgical sites, a urine catheter was also there, an 'NBM' board was hanging on the saline stand near the bed. After five days, the tubes were removed and I was advised to consume soups and easy-to-digest food. Suddenly I developed nausea and felt like eating nothing. Nilambari forcibly used to give me something to eat saying, "How will you recuperate your lost energy if you don't eat?" Her logic was right but I started vomiting whatever little I ate. The antacids did not work. Finally, a tube was inserted through the nose and throat and the acid was removed. I felt better but as soon as the tube was removed, the hyperacidity started once again. It took doctors three days to bring my health back to normal. My stay in KDAH got extended by three days and I came home after twelve days of admission.

Before discharge, Dr Ankur Shah visited with oncologist, Dr Shastry, who said, "Mr Sathe, since we have seen that secondaries have developed in your body, it is decided that you will be administered six chemotherapy sessions starting from 3 May 2013. You will need to get admitted for three days. The medicine will be administered through I.V. every three weeks. Chemo is necessary as a preventive measure." There was no reason to argue or question. I needed to be ready to face the line of treatment and I was ready for the same.

We should consider every operation or a long-drawn treatment as an examination. Just as before appearing for the exam, we study hard and prepare physically and mentally, similarly I tried to study as much about colorectal or colon cancer on the Internet as possible. On reading some of the research papers, one is likely to be afraid and lose heart. In one such paper, I read that seventy per cent of the patients with colon cancer had secondaries developed on either the liver or prostate. The life span, on an average, of such patients was up to three years. Many patients died of organ failure due to weakness and infection. Nilambari used to deter me from reading such material, but I used to tell her, I cannot predict my death. As a student of Statistics, I know how an average is calculated. There are always some values below the average and some above the average level. Jokingly I once asked her, "What do you think about your husband, he is average, above average or below average?" She proudly replied, "You are not just above average, but you are outstanding." So laughingly I said, "See if three years is average, six may be above average and outstanding will certainly be of any value greater than six. Don't worry. Like a marathon runner who doesn't give up, I too will fight out the cancer. It's always better to be knowledgeable and die than without knowing the cause of it."

After a reasonable recovery, I started reading about chemotherapy, its uses, side effects etc. I knew for sure that out of hundreds of drugs used for chemotherapy, it's very difficult to predict which suits your body most. It all depends on the judgment of the oncologist. Dr Shastry was a senior oncologist so I had no doubt on his judgement and competence. When I asked him beforehand about the medicine he was going to give me, he said, "I will decide based on the progress you make in the next two months after your discharge from the hospital."

As per advice, I got admitted to KDAH on Friday, the 3 May 2013 after office hours. LIC AMC office used to be closed every Saturday and Sunday. So I told the doctor that I would get admitted for the chemotherapy either on Friday after office hours or on Saturday morning. Dr Shastry then explained to me what chemotherapy was all about, how it prevents growth of cancer cells, what precautions should be taken, what are its side effects etc. He also informed me that I would be administered some medicine through I.V. before and after injecting the chemotherapy drug which will reduce its side-effects. The chemotherapy drug that he decided on was called Avastin and the quantity each time was five hundred millilitres. He told me, "It would be injected very slowly, maybe a drop of it every fifteen seconds. It may take thirty-six to forty hours for five hundred millilitres of medicine to be injected through I.V. When injected slowly, it will prevent growth of new blood cells that feed tumours. It is called 'Targeted Chemotherapy'. My body was quite responsive to the drug and the first session was over without any complications. I came back home on Monday. I was feeling thoroughly exhausted. Walking even ten steps was difficult for me. I took complete rest on Monday, got up only at 8:00 am on Tuesday but went to the office. I was determined not to stay at home, unless it was a must. My legs used to tremble but I used to walk with the support of the walls. The first week post-chemo was very difficult to pull through. I used to have no energy left after coming from office. The second week onwards, I began taking a morning walk, increasing roughly 100 steps everyday and by the end of the third week, I would walk for about three kilometres before getting admitted for the next chemo session. Fortunately, the common side-effects of chemo like abdominal pain, poor appetite, constipation, upper respiratory infection, nausea and vomiting were generally not observed in me. However, the White Blood Cell (WBC) count was steadily coming down. Loss of hair was not a problem for me as I had already lost considerable hair on my head and was almost bald.

Nilambari was taking care of my high-protein diet. I had fresh coconut water in the morning and ragi payasam. My friend and batchmate, Saroj stayed on the fourth floor in the same building. Her mother used to send me chicken soup every evening. As I was unable to eat much in one go, Nilambari used to feed me in small quantities of pomegranate juice, sago kheer and other dishes which I liked. All such care and personal attention to what I ate helped me recuperate faster. I lost eight to ten kilograms of weight during the four months of chemo which ended in mid-August 2013. The WBC level count before the last chemo was just above the minimum permissible level. Had it been below by a few hundreds, the chemo would have been postponed. PET CT scan was done fifteen days after the last chemotherapy cycle. The report was normal. As per protocol, the CT of abdomen and pelvis done in November 2013 was normal. My appetite improved, my weight increased and I started going for morning walk of five kilometres. Internally, I never felt any discomfort.

After the six cycles of chemotherapy, a period of almost a year was over and my PET CT in February followed by CT in May 2014 were normal. I thought that the cancer cells in my body have bid me a goodbye permanently. But that was not the case. The PET CT scan done in August 2014 showed metastasis on the fifth and seventh segments of the liver. Fortunately, the report didn't mention the growth of cancer on other parts of the body. On reading the report, my heart, for the first time, sank. Despite surgery and chemotherapy, cancer erupted again. I thought to myself, maybe the drug Avastin used for chemotherapy was not as effective or perhaps the oncologist's judgement of choosing Avastin for me was wrong. When I spoke with Dr Ankur Shah about it, he said, "Mr Sathe, we can infer that the drug was effective from the fact that cancer has not spread to other organs of the body and it continues to be localized to liver. There is no option but to remove the infected part of liver again by surgery. If you want, you may consult another onco-surgeon."

Dr Sanjeevanee Kelkar, who was my cousin's wife, saw the report and advised me to consult Dr Mahesh Goel of Tata Memorial Cancer Hospital (TMCH). He saw the reports and the medical history and said, "Mr Sathe, out of three options namely surgery, chemotherapy and radiation, I will advise you surgery first and if required, chemotherapy later. I can operate on you but TMCH being a general hospital, your waiting period will be longer and I won't advise you to wait long for the surgery. Post-surgery care is, of course, better in private hospitals, but the charges are also higher than our hospital. If you can afford to get surgery done in a private hospital at the hands of a good liver surgeon, get it done quickly."

Dr Ankur Shah, in the meanwhile, left KDAH and joined Raheja Hospital. Hence within eight days, to be precise on 14 August 2014 the third cancer surgery was done. My friend Mr S K Roy had, by then became Chairman, LIC, and he had sent my history and reports to his friend who was an onco-surgeon in Kolkata. His friend advised, "It being the third cancer surgery, it is not easy. Moreover, the removal of metastasis on the seventh segment of the liver needs a great amount of skill on part of the surgeon. If the surgery can't be completed within the given time-frame, it will be advisable to close the surgery rather than it turning out to be fatal to the patient."

On hearing this, I met Dr Ankur Shah. He said, "Yes, this surgery is difficult, no doubt, but I am confident that I will be able to do it well."

I said, "Doctor, I didn't tell you earlier, but my father had a kidney stone surgery done in 1961 in J J Hospital and he died on the operation table itself. I don't want to die like him."

He laughed and said, "Mr Sathe, in the last forty to fifty years, medical science has developed a lot. Rest assured, in case I am not able to finish the surgery in the given time and I find that the situation is going out of control, I will ensure that you will live with cancer rather than dying without it. I will give nobody the chance to say, 'Operation was successful, but the patient died'.

I gained confidence with his words which were quite reassuring. I requested him to allow my sister-in-law, Dr Sanjeevanee Kelkar, who was earlier trained at TMCH for two years, to be present at the time of surgery. He said, "He would request the Hospital Management to allow her to be present at the time of surgery."

On the family front, Kaustubh had left his job in Maruti Suzuki and had joined Indian Institute of Management, Bangalore for Post Graduate Diploma in Management. He had family accommodation in the hostel and hence, Saylee, his wife also shifted to Bangalore. He was keen on coming to Mumbai to be there during my hospitalization but Himanshu asked him to focus on his studies and told him that he had taken ten days leave to support his mother during my hospitalization. Tai and Sudhir had come for fifteen days and were of great support. All the blood tests and other reports were normal, ECG was within normal limits, BP was within limits and I got admitted to Raheja Hospital on 13 August 2014. By then our Mediclaim limit had increased to ₹10 lakh and as such, I was able to occupy a Special Room which was a great comfort to Nilambari and to me as well. My sister-in-law, Dr Sanjeevanee Kelkar reached the Hospital at 7:00 am directly from Pune to be present at the time of surgery. On seeing her, my confidence level went up and I was sure that I would come out successfully. I was shifted to the Operation Theatre at 8:00 am and I later came to know that Dr Sanjeevanee Kelkar came out of OT at about 2:00 pm to inform all those present in my room that the surgery went off well. When I was shifted to the ICU, she again saw me and told Nilambari, "Nilesh is lucky. I have done and seen many such surgeries in the past, but the surgery done by Dr Ankur Shah today was simply outstanding. Nilesh is in safe hands. He will recover fast."

I regained consciousness the next day. When the doctors in the ICU noticed that I was awake they made arrangements to shift me to the room. A gurney was placed close to my bed in the ICU and four attendants were to lift me from my bed and shift me to the gurney. I noticed it and said, "Don't lift me. I will move myself slowly and shift to the gurney." I did so slowly. An attendant who was observing me said, "Within twenty-four hours of surgery, such movement of the patient is generally not seen. Your confidence is remarkable."

I don't know, but to be honest, the first time I regained consciousness, I felt quite energetic and I felt that my body is not going to allow the cancer cells to grow again. I am cancer free now. I do not know how I had so much confidence after three cancer surgeries. But frankly, on the second day itself, I started walking in the corridor of the hospital. The CT scan report, after eight days of surgery showed no traces of cancer cells and I was discharged from the hospital on the ninth day without any post- surgery complications.

The doctor advised me to follow the protocol of CT and PET CT scan every six months for the next two years and thereafter, once in a year. I was not prescribed any medicines or tonics. I came home and joined the office after ten days of rest. In case of cancer, a patient either has cancer or is cancer-free. There is no stage in between. I was cancer-free for sure.

By then, I had completed two years as CEO in LIC Nomura Mutual Fund AMC. The fund performance had improved. The AMC came out of the red after many years. The efforts put in by me had started yielding results. The AUM crossed ₹10,000 crore. In the top twenty mutual funds on AUM basis, it was ranked first in growth rate, showing growth of over ninety per cent in two years.

When I joined in 2012, there were four Japanese on the rolls of AMC, one was, Mr Kurozu, Chief Strategist, the other was the Chief Investment Officer, the third was a Fund Manager and the fourth was a Research Associate. It was my first experience of working with Japanese employees. Japanese do not open up easily. After they started liking my style of working, Mr Kurozu, slowly started telling me reasons for their request to replace the earlier CEO. In order to give a professional look to the AMC, Mr Vijayan, the then Chairman of LIC had forged a Joint Venture agreement with Nomura Group of Japan offering them thirty-five per cent stake in the company. This was probably not liked by the then CEO of the AMC. So right from day one, the Japanese employees got a raw deal at his hands. Out of the annual salary of ₹7.5 crore of all the two hundred and sixty-five employees of LIC AMC, only the four Japanese together were drawing a salary of ₹2.5 crore. This was a regular point of dissent. I was told that the then CEO often used to say, "Our LIC employees on deputation do the same work as you do at just ten per cent of your salary. You don't deserve such a high salary. We have made a mistake by partnering with you. You want to take over our AMC." Mr Kurozu once told me, "I had to seek the CEO's appointment before meeting him. I was made to wait for long. The relations were never cordial. I informed LIC Chairman Mr Mehrotra, about it and requested him to replace the CEO."

I realized why the Chairman wanted me to head the mutual fund. During my three years as CEO, I gave due respect to the Japanese officers. It's not that we always agreed with each and every issue but those were sorted out with mutual understanding and respect. In the first year, we registered a loss of ₹2.75 crore. I told Mr Kurozu one day, "The research reports of the listed companies are shared with our Japanese counterparts in Singapore. Can we charge them fees for the same?"

He appreciated the idea and we had tele-conference with Nomura Singapore. They insisted on 100 research reports every year for ₹2.5 crore. We agreed and insisted on quarterly evaluation and pay out, which they agreed and we could increase our fee-based income by ₹2.5 crore which was almost matching with the salary outgo of the four Japanese employees. I had read somewhere that most joint ventures failed, not due to financial reasons but because of culture related issues. I therefore started my daily morning meeting at 10:00 am for twenty to thirty minutes over a cup of tea with two senior Japanese officers and COO and CMO who were Indians. The meeting helped us come closer and iron out our differences. We used to discuss anything and everything under the sun, right from Indian festivals to sushi. One day, as it started raining, the cable operator displayed the message on TV screen 'Sorry for the interruption'. I asked Mr Kurozu, "Does this happen in Japan too?"

The Japanese will never give a sudden reaction. They will think twice before they speak. After searching for the right words, he said with a serious face, "I think, it used to happen when I was in college twenty-five years ago." He could have said, "India is using the technology which was used by Japan twenty-five years ago", but he gave a polite reply to my question. During Navratri celebrations, the Japanese were amazed to find most of the female employees in our office wearing different coloured attire based on the specific colour of that day, on each day of the nine days of celebrations. Mr Kurozu used to request them daily to stand in a group and click a picture. One day he said, "Mr Sathe, every shade of green was seen today. In Japan we wear white, ash, or light brown colour shirts and dresses. Even the buildings have light ash or white colour. Indians have a great sense of colours."

Initially the office timing was 9:30 am to 5:30 pm with a forty-five minute lunch break. Mr Kurozu once said, "Mr Sathe, when the stock market opens at 9:00 am, why can we not start our office at 9:00 am? All the other mutual fund offices start at 9:00 am and have forty hours of work per week." What he said was right. I took approval from the Board to change the office timing from 9:00 am to 5:30 pm with a thirty minute lunch break. Of course, even before that, the Japanese officers used to reach office at 8:30 am, the liftman used to report at 9:00 am but they never grumbled or requested me to ask the liftman to report at 8:30 am, they would climb one hundred steps to reach the office on the fourth floor.

The Japanese CIO was very methodical. He set up the front office, mid office and the back office. Mobile phones were strictly prohibited in the Dealing Room. No equity investment was made without a research report. I never saw him leaving office before 7:00 pm. Due to his systematic working, performance of various schemes improved, generating alpha over the benchmark index.

The Japanese are always very eager to learn new things. Once, Nilambari invited them for dinner. It was their first experience of having dinner at the residence of any LIC officer. Nilambari had herself cooked vegetarian food that day. They were astonished to see how the *roti (phulka)* gets filled with hot air to its brim. After dinner, they requested Nilambari to demonstrate to them how she makes *phulkas*. Each of them tried their hand on making one or two *phulkas*. They liked the home made mixed vegetable pickle. Nilambari gave them a bottle of pickle each. Mr S K Roy, Chairman, and I were invited by Nomura to visit their office in Tokyo. We were their guests for a week. Their hospitality was unmatched. We travelled by bullet train to Kyoto where they showed us the Nomura Garden which is the property of the founder of the company. We had lunch at Tokyo Tower. It was a memorable trip.

I used to visit at least one corporate client every week along with our CIO or Fund Manager to showcase to them our investment strategy. Generally, such visits are done only by CIO or Fund Manager. A CEO of a reputed company which regularly used to invest in our Liquid Fund Scheme once said, "Mr Sathe, let me tell you honestly that you are the first CEO of any mutual fund who has come and met me in my office." Such visits helped me to learn the language of Fund Managers. It also helped me to understand, when and where to invest, how to evaluate fund performance etc. I said to myself, "My forefathers used to visit five houses daily and chant, '*Om Bhavati Bhiksham Dehi*', which means begging alms as a livelihood. If that was the order of the day why should I feel shy of visiting corporate houses and asking for funds?" It yielded results.

I started a Performance Appraisal and Bell Curve method of evaluation of performance. Similarly I obtained approval from the Board for leave policy, LTC policy, dress code, confidentiality policy etc. and implemented them. Employees who scored below three on a scale of five in their annual appraisal were brought under Performance Improvement Programme (PIP) and out of which those who failed to show improvement, were shown the door. In 2012 when I joined, there were over one hundred and fifty officers from LIC on deputation at various offices of the LIC AMC. In three years, I reduced this number to just three, including me. The Fund Managers of insurance companies follow a strategy of 'Buy and Hold'. They don't churn their portfolio regularly to book profit. In a mutual fund, however, the Fund Managers have to be agile and active to show better performance each day and to be in Top Ten performers. This being the fundamental difference in approach, I found that the best Fund Managers from LIC were unable to show good performance in LIC AMC. I sent them back to LIC, not because they were incapable or incompetent, but because they were a 'Square peg in round hole'. I recruited Research Associates, Fund Managers, CIO, CMO from the open market by paying them market-based salaries. The number of employees drastically reduced from two hundred and sixty-five to one hundred and seventy in the three years but still the AUM increased by over one hundred and thirty percent. I had a satisfying tenure in LIC Nomura MF AMC. It gave me new insight in managing a private company.

One day, I came across an advertisement released by the Department of Financial Services about recruitment for the post of 'Whole time Member (Life)' in Insurance Regulatory and Development Authority of India (IRDAI). ED in LIC is equivalent to Joint Secretary in the Government of India hierarchy. The post of Whole Time Member in IRDAI was equivalent to the post of Additional Secretary or Managing Director of LIC. My qualification and experience of over twenty-five years in the insurance field satisfactorily met the requirements and hence I decided to apply for the same. Interviews were conducted in February 2015. There were at least two officers senior to me who had applied. But I had faced the interview confidently and was sure to get selected.

In the meantime, after Jaipur High Court set aside all the charges included under the Atrocities Act and criminal charge of abetment to suicide, I requested the LIC Chairman to restore the fifty-six days of leave I had taken to remain in hiding, as per his advice. Mr Mehrotra showed magnanimity in considering my request and my leave was restored.

Kaustubh completed his PGDM from IIM Bangalore and was recruited by a consulting firm named Servion, in Chennai. We attended his convocation ceremony at IIM Bangalore and I was happy that both of my sons had a degree in Management. Himanshu had done his MBA from ICFAI and had completed a few more certifications like PMP and Six Sigma. Thus, both my children were more qualified than me. What else does a father want?

By March 2015 I had two more years to retire from LIC and since I had completed a tenure of three years in LIC Nomura MF AMC, I was due for posting back to LIC as ED of a department. The result of my interview was awaited. Had I gotten selected in IRDAI, I would have got four more years to retire as the retirement age in IRDAI was sixty two.

I met Mr S K Roy, Chairman, in the first week of April 2015 to brief him about the performance of LIC Nomura MF AMC. The AUM had gone up in -three years from ₹5400 crore to over ₹13,000 crore, showing a growth of one hundred and forty per cent. The mutual fund industry, during that period, had grown by forty per cent. Our AMC was one of the sixteen AMCs out of forty-five in India which showed profit in 2014-15. When I took charge in 2012, only six out of our thirty scheme's performance was above the bench-mark. In March 2015 all the schemes were giving return to investors above the bench-mark, thereby generating alpha. He expressed his satisfaction over my performance. I requested him to allow me to continue in the same position till my retirement in 2017, but also making it clear that I would accept any assignment of his choice. He just smiled and said nothing.

Finally, when the Transfer List of EDs was announced, my name was not there but my batch mate and dear friend, Ms Saroj Dikhale was shown posted as CMO in LIC Nomura MF AMC. When I met Mr Roy, he said, "Nilesh, In case you get selected as Member, IRDAI, Saroj will replace you as CEO, as such, till that time, I want you to train her since she has no previous experience of working in the Investment Department, nor does she have a Commerce background. Saroj joined LIC Nomura MF AMC immediately. She was intelligent and a very good HR person. As such, it was not difficult for her to fit into the position of CEO.

On 15 June 2015 in the evening, the Department of Personnel and Training (DoPT), Government of India, posted a notification on their website appointing me as 'Whole time Member (Life)' IRDAI. This news spread like a wildfire and till late in the night, I got phone calls one after the other, congratulating me on my selection. I met Mr S K Roy, Chairman, LIC and thanked him for his support. He was very happy that I was selected. I told him that I would decide whether to join or not, only after meeting Dr Ankur Shah for his opinion about my health.

I met Dr Shah, informed him of my selection and explained to him how the selection was important and prestigious. I briefed him about how challenging the new assignment would be. I also told him that it would double my salary and my retirement age would go up by two years. He replied, "Mr Sathe, I would not have left Mumbai to join Hyderabad even if someone would have offered me a ten-fold increase in pay." I said, "Doctor, by the grace of God, money is not a problem. Children are well settled; my wife is not employed and she is ready to move with me to Hyderabad if I join. Taking into account the present state of my health, please tell me if I should accept or decline the offer. I will go by your advice."

He said, "Mr Sathe, what does your inner voice say?" I instantly replied, "I should accept."

Dr Shah said, "Then say 'Yes' and proceed." As far as the present condition of your health is concerned, you are totally cancer-free. What will happen tomorrow, no one can predict. Follow the protocol, remain cheerful, as you always are. In case cancer erupts again, it may erupt without considering the location of your stay. We will cross that bridge when we get there. Don't worry."

I thanked him. Before I left him, he said, "Mr Sathe, when I write my memoir, I am going to reserve a page for you. At the age of fifty-eight, after three major cancer surgeries and six sessions of chemotherapy, you are ready to venture to a new place where you have never been before and do something that you have never done before. It is simply incredible. You have an indomitable fighting spirit. Do you remember, before your third cancer surgery, I had taken your consent to discuss your case in a conference of surgeons? Today let me disclose to you a secret. After showing your reports and medical history, I had asked the surgeons if I should go ahead with your third cancer surgery. Not a single surgeon was in favour of it. One fellow even said, "Let him die peacefully." Despite this, I performed the surgery looking at your will power and spirit to fight cancer and it was successful. God is with you. You go ahead. My best wishes to you for your new assignment."

Normally, a three months' notice is required to be given for Voluntary Retirement from LIC. As I was asked by the Government to join soon, I requested a waiver of the notice period and requested the Chairman of LIC to relieve me on 30 June 2015 so that I may join IRDAI Hyderabad on 1 July 2015. During the two weeks' notice period after my selection, I prepared Saroj mentally to step into my shoes as CEO from 1 July 2015.

I never imagined that my departure day from LIC would be so sudden. I had to wind up things in Mumbai, inform relatives and acquaintances, which I did. I received a warm farewell from LIC Nomura MF AMC and also from LIC.

We took the morning flight on 1 July 2015 from Mumbai to Hyderabad to start a new era in our lives. After boarding the aircraft, I said, "Nilambari, you brought change in my life. What I am today, is only because of you. I was a clerk in the Bank of India. It was only because of your persuasion that I applied for the post of AAO in LIC and rose to the highest level. You stood by me like a rock in all my difficult days. You sacrificed your career and followed me wherever I was posted. My mother laid the foundation of my character and you built a dome over it. All the credit for whatever I have achieved in life goes to you."

I could see the contentment on her face. Her eyes were closed, but she had a smile on her face. She whispered in my ears, "Stay strong and never give up. Ever." The flight took off for a new destination. A new journey had begun.

Lessons Learnt...

- Recovery is faster when there is someone to pay attention to you lovingly.
- Have an indomitable fighting spirit.
- Stay strong and Never Give Up!

About the Author

Nilesh Sathe was Member, IRDAI Hyderabad from 2015 to 2019 during which he headed the Life Insurance Department along with Legal, IT, HR and Admin for all the four years.

Before joining IRDAI, he was Director and CEO of LIC Nomura Mutual Fund Asset Management Company for a period of three years. Before that he headed the Northern Zone of LIC of India as Zonal Manager, New Delhi as in-charge of Marketing and Administration. He held various positions in LIC of India, such as Executive Director of a Marketing Channel, Chief (Pension & Group Schemes Dept.) and Senior Divisional Manager of two Divisions in Mumbai.

He worked with Bank of India and Canara Bank for over five years before joining LIC of India as a Direct Recruit Officer. He brings with him a rich experience of over four decades in the Banking, Insurance and the Mutual Fund industry. He is a rank holder with distinction in M.Com from Nagpur University. He is also a Certified Associate of Indian Institute of Bankers.

During his tenure as Member in IRDAI, He was a member of the Implementation Committee of International Association of Insurance Supervisors (IAIS) and represented India in Basel

(Switzerland), Morocco, Budapest, Moscow, Singapore etc. He was also Member of Asian Insurance Forum and represented India at Manila, Bangkok, Taipei etc.

He has recently been appointed as Advisor (Finance) by National Highways Authority India to help them garner funds from FIIs, World Bank, ADB, pension funds and from DIIs.

He is an independent Director on the Board of Mahindra Manulife Mutual Fund.